"You know, I don't like yc ... er
on the *Mary Tyler Moore* ... n
Caddyshack."

West was on a roll. Ronald Ryan was speechless. What was this man talking about?

"Just leave Oregon and go back to LA," said West.

"I live in Oregon now," said Ryan. "I've got a plan for the beaches. That's what this is all about. You and the socialist teacher, Love."

"You have no idea where you live. We're going to teach you. There will be flesh," said West.

Hey, thought West, *that sounded pretty good, pretty hard-boiled, pretty classic detective fiction. There will be flesh! And sand! Sounds very Tyrone Power. I'll be sure to mention it to Love. He could use the help, seeing that no one publishes him except himself.*

"I'm getting security," said Ryan. He got up and dashed out of the bar.

West was gone when security arrived. Before leaving the resort, he carved another sentence on Ryan's Hummer. It gleamed beautifully in the light after he pissed on it: "THE GREAT BIRTHRIGHT LIVES!"

An hour later, Ryan read the scratches. He was livid. He wanted to call a lackey and scream. But his phone was dead, deader than every soul of every Republican Senator from the 11 states of the former Confederacy.

Ryan got into the Hummer, muttering to himself: "Great birthright? What's that? Who are these people? These Oregonians?"

THE GREAT BIRTHRIGHT

(AN OREGON NOVEL)

Nestucca Spit Press | Astoria, Oregon

w w w . n e s t u c c a s p i t p r e s s . c o m

An independent Oregon press publishing books about Oregon

Printed in Newport, Oregon by Dave and Pioneer Printing

Book design by Amira Shagaga

Copy edited by Erin Labasan

Cover art by Cindy Popp

Nestucca Spit Press was established in 2003 to publish books about Oregon.
All books are printed in Oregon and distributed exclusively at independent
bookstores, in taverns, through the website, and at live events.

OTHER NESTUCCA SPIT PRESS BOOKS BY MATT LOVE

*Let it Pour: An Unconventional Drinking Guide to
the North and Central Oregon Coast | www.letitpour.net* (2002)

*Grasping Wastrels Vs Beaches Forever Inc.:
Covering the Fights for the Soul of the Oregon Coast* (2003)

The Far Out Story of Vortex 1 (2004)

*Red Hot and Rollin': A Retrospection of the Portland Trail Blazers'
1976-77 Championship Season* (2007)

Citadel of the Spirit: Oregon's Sesquicentennial Anthology (2008)

Super Sunday in Newport: Notes From My First Year in Town (2009)

Gimme Refuge: The Education of a Caretaker (2010)

The Teaching Maxims of Karl Love (2011)

*Love & The Green Lady: Meditations on the Yaquina Bay Bridge,
Oregon's Crown Jewel of Socialism* (2011)

*Sometimes a Great Movie: Paul Newman, Ken Kesey
and the Filming of the Great Oregon Novel* (2012)

Of Walking in Rain (2013)

*Rose City Heist: A True Crime Portland Tale of Sex,
Gravy, Jewelry and Almost Rock and Roll* (2014)

A Nice Piece of Astoria: A Narrative Guide (2015)

FOR MATT KRAMER, SONNY, AUDREY AND ROSE

CHAPTER 1
A SHIFTING SHADOW

It is exceedingly rare when authentic legal decisions, including a blistering dissent from a dyspeptic US Supreme Court justice, open a work of pseudo pulp historical environmental detective socialist metafiction. In fact, it's never happened before.

So, here it goes.

Cannon Beach motel owner Bill Hay challenged Oregon's 1967 Beach Bill in state court. The legislative battle that culminated with the passage of this landmark law started with Hay trying to privatize the beach in front of his property. There was no way he wasn't going to fight creeping socialism. Can't let the people win if it means the greater good for Oregon. Capitalism is like that.

In 1969, the Oregon Supreme Court upheld the state constitutionality of the Beach Bill in *Thornton v. Hay* by advancing an interesting legal theory:

> *The most cogent basis for the decision in this case is the English doctrine of custom. Strictly construed, prescription applies only to the specific tract of land before the court, and doubtful prescription cases could fill the courts for years with tract-by-tract litigation. An established custom, on the other hand, can be proven with reference to a larger region. Ocean-front lands from the northern to the southern border of the state ought to be treated uniformly...the custom of the people*

of Oregon to use the dry-sand area of the beaches for public recreational purposes meets every one of Blackstone's requisites...the custom of the inhabitants of Oregon and of visitors in the state to use the dry sand as a public recreation area is so notorious that notice of the custom . . . must be presumed.

In other words, because Oregonians had been freely recreating on their ocean beaches for so long, they'd earned a permanent easement to keep using them. Squatters' rights!

Hay packed it in after losing the Oregon Supreme Court decision. And that should have been that. The free and uninterrupted use thereof forever—from Hammond to Brookings. Drop dead private beaches.

But it wasn't. A quarter century later, another Cannon Beach property owner challenged the constitutionality of the Beach Bill. Irving and Jeanette Stevens had owned a beachfront parcel since 1957 and in 1989 wanted to build a seawall to protect it. The city of Cannon Beach denied them a permit contending the Stevens' proposed structure in the dry sands areas was disallowed by the Beach Bill and its concomitant regulations. The Stevenses sued the city, claiming the taking was in violation of the Fifth and Fourteenth Amendments. They wanted to be compensated for not polluting public recreation space.

In 1994, the case made it all the way to the US Supreme Court but a writ of certiorari was denied in a 7-2 decision. Justice Antonin Scalia wrote the dissent:

In Thornton v. Hay, the Supreme Court of Oregon appears to have misread Blackstone in applying the law of custom to the entire Oregon coast...To say that this case raises a seri-

ous Fifth Amendment takings issue is an understatement. The issue is serious in the sense that it involves a holding of questionable constitutionality; and it is serious in the sense that the land-grab (if there is one) may run the entire length of the Oregon coast... Particularly in light of the utter absence of recorded support for the crucial factual determinations in that case, whether the Oregon Supreme Court chooses to treat it as having established a "custom" applicable to Cannon Beach alone, or one applicable to all "dry-sand" beach in the State, petitioners must be afforded an opportunity to make out their constitutional claim by demonstrating that the asserted custom is pretextual. If we were to find for petitioners on this point, we would not only set right a procedural injustice, but would hasten the clarification of Oregon substantive law that casts a shifting shadow upon federal constitutional rights the length of the State. I would grant the petition for certiorari with regard to the due process claim.

A shifting shadow.

Who would have thought that a medieval, self-flagellating, flat earth, reactionary like Scalia would insert some alliterative hard-boiled pulp fiction flourishes like *shifting shadow* in a sleazy, scumbag Supreme Court opinion that took the side of a sliver of private property over limitless public good?

Well, he did, and apparently without any irony whatsoever, because as anyone who actually pays attention to what's happening in America knows, Scalia and his gilded one-percent dark ilk are the true *shifting shadow* that threatens a permanent blackout of participatory democracy and a prosperous middle class. They need to be taken down, hard, if only the American people would wake up and do it.

What this horribly written dissent was trying to say: Oregon should have ruled on the Stevens matter and every disputed beachfront parcel case by case, inch by inch, and not have applied the rule of custom the entire length of the Oregon Coast.

Scalia may have represented the corporate antichrist to all American progressive causes, but he was no fool. He sowed a demon seed with his dissent, undoubtedly biding his time until the prevailing political winds blew in a more favorably lucrative direction. Scalia, the windbag, was now the juggernaut of a private wind machine with plenty of force to blow the Beach Bill deep into the historical abyss.

The moment was primed for the Scalias and their fiendish allies to inject their private property rights ideology into Oregon, confront the Beach Bill, and have it declared unconstitutional by the current syndicate that comprised the majority of the Supreme Court. That, in turn, would unleash the developers and destroyers in the dry sands areas to reclaim it as exclusively their own fiefdom. Next would come fences, seawalls, boardwalks, espresso stands, food carts, hourly rates, cabanas, corporate sponsorship, more riprap, ads on riprap, NO TRESPASSING signs, security guards, video surveillance, floodlights, Kenny G or techno on outdoor speakers. No dogs. No bonfires and guitars. No driftwood forts and smoking pot. No beer and naked dashes into the ocean in broad daylight. No poor people allowed.

An upholstered, prudish, mercantile, privatized hell in Oregon…and only a 5-4 vote away.

The Roberts Court wouldn't deny a writ of certiorari this time. They'd fast track any case that provided any shred of opportunity to overthrow the people and dogs and driftwood forts and cede control to money-men, conglomerates and umbrella users. They'd overturn the Beach Bill with such sanctimonious glee that within a generation Oregon's coastline would resemble New Jersey's, and the hallowed names of Oswald West, Tom McCall and Matt Kramer would fade from memory, gone forever except in the minds of crank writers and prophets toiling in the sandy wilderness, writing and preaching about an era so distant that it might have been Middle Earth or the New Deal.

If that happened, Oregon was dead.

This was Ronald Ryan's master nefarious scheme all along. He was out to steal Oregon's great birthright, its publicly-owned beaches.

CHAPTER 2
THE MAD DOG

It was a dark and stormy Tuesday night in late November, the Season of Rain as opposed to the witch. Maybe both. That's when the fear starts, that's when you sell the juice on the Oregon Coast.

A shot rang out inside the Mad Dog Country Tavern, from a black and white portable television that dangled above the bar and couldn't possibly broadcast a digital signal, but was. Five Oregon Tavern Age (OTA = appearing anywhere from 40-70 years old) men were watching an episode of *Perry Mason* with the sound off and talking in monotone double and triple profane negatives. They loved their *Perry Mason* in the Mad Dog and always speculated about whether Perry ever nailed Della. The consensus was he had. Every other day. They also loved watching *Body Heat* with Kathleen Turner and William Hurt on VHS movie night. The scene with the wet spot staining her sheer dress drove them weakly stiff. The film should have been shot in black and white back in 1981, and, well, now it was, because the Mad Dog had a way of rectifying technological wrongs.

The Mad Dog was like that, old, but not knowingly retro. No regular customer even knew what the word "retro" meant. To them, Westerns were still popular culture; Shane was Shane, and Louis L'Amour was a dusty noir writer of merit. Stephen King who?

Rainier signs decorated the Mad Dog's faux paneled walls. The regulars didn't know they were vintage. To them, there was no such thing as vintage connected to any aspect of Rainier. Nor did the regulars

think twice about the faded blue industrial carpet that someone had rescued from a dump in Waldport and installed for free beer for a year. The one noteworthy piece of décor was a set of six homemade shell-shaped lights encrusted with all manner of tiny crustacean life hanging over the bar. No one had the slightest idea who made them.

There was one baseboard heater in the Mad Dog and one pool table. No one ever played pool but the table was infrequently a conversation item. It had a sticker with a telephone number to call for repair on the table, 666-6666. The one regular who drunkenly dialed the number (it rang but no one answered) died in his sleep a day later and no one ever called the number again.

The tavern got its name in the 1960s when a log rigged up like a teeter totter with seatbelts rested near the entrance. From time to time, two OTA men would challenge each other, buckle up at both ends, and then consume a bottle of Mad Dog while teeter tottering. The winner remained sitting upright. Then he unbuckled and went to work. Some 40 years later, his predecessors worked exactly the same jobs (for roughly a third of the pay, adjusted for inflation): concrete, dry walling, framing, scrap metal, roofing, firewood. Most of the OTA Men had one-syllable first names like Ed, Sam, Frank, Fred, Bill. One of them was named Toad. Toad loved telling the same story over and over again to anyone who would listen or was asleep at the bar. He always told it in the third person like Caesar or Norman Mailer. It went like this:

> *It was 1976, Bicentennial summer, and Walter Cronkite still delivered the CBS Evening News. Toad and some friends were driving from Tampa to Panama City Beach in a Camaro convertible. The temperature was a hundred and nine degrees. Chicks in bikinis were hanging out the sides and everyone was drinking Miller High Life in bottles. They ran out of beer and didn't have any money for more. Toad was dying of thirst and saw the last bottle of Miller rolling on the floor of the Camaro. He drank it and fried his mouth. The beer was a hundred degrees, a deep fried Miller. That was the last High Life Toad ever drank.*

All the Mad Dog regulars had stories like Toad's. If only there was an Oregon writer who divined gold in their value and wanted to write them up. When it came to storytelling or bullshitting at the bar, none of the regulars ever uttered the word *whatever* in a conversation, although some of them had beat the shit out of younger co-workers shirking on the job who had. *Whatever* hurts when a fist smashes into your face while you're texting on your phone when you're supposed to be troweling concrete.

Fortified wine was off the menu these days. Today, the tavern only served cheap Pacific Northwest lagers formerly brewed in the Pacific Northwest by union men, jug California wine popular in the 1970s, and rotgut champagne for two bucks a glass. There was no craft beer, no liquor, no video poker, no Oregon lottery of any kind, no ATM, no credit cards accepted, no dartboard, no jukebox, no NFL Prime Ticket. Wi-Fi? What the fuck was that?

There wasn't even a kitchen. The only food came courtesy of plastic bags, a microwave and plastic jars showcasing various neon pickled grotesqueries with names like Big Daddy, Hot Mama, Yellow Doggie. For most of the Mad Dog regulars, these grotesqueries constituted a majority of their daily nutritional intake. That, and all the beer, fresh crab and salmon they caught and ate not more than a stone's throw from the parking lot. Caught and ate while waterlogged drunk.

If the regulars wanted a smoke, they went outside to a grove of cedar trees stunted by wind and cigarette smoke. There was a patio with a picnic table and horseshoe pit nearby, too. The last time they'd played horseshoes, a man ended up in the hospital.

For some unknown reason, the Mad Dog had a red and white stucco and wood Tudor façade, the only one of its kind on the Oregon Coast, or in hell. The tavern's other noteworthy décor was a number of Polaroid collages hanging in macramé frames. Virtually everyone pictured in the collages was drunk at some Mad Dog event, like the Fourth of July pig roast or the Christmas potluck and gift exchange. These folks were also all dead. There were dogs in the collages, too. Most of them were still alive, perhaps because they never ate the pickled grotesqueries. One of the dogs, Chet, a hulking black lab, spent most of his time sprawled on the carpeted floor in the middle of the tavern. It wasn't clear who owned him. He just sort of drifted home with a different regular every night at closing and then returned at nine in the morning when the Mad Dog reopened.

Sometimes women appeared in the Mad Dog. They were OTA, too. Sometimes these men and women fornicated together, but to reveal any of that dank intimacy would provide gradations of sex and a modicum of romance to this story—kind of—and this is a celibate pseudo pulp detective novel, so forget it.

Outside, rain ripped across the Yaquina River and through the trailer park adjacent to the tavern. It was rain with intent, personality, mood, command. It was the type of rain that made you want to drink yourself to death or write a book about people drinking themselves to death. There was very little in between these two existential fates. Rain on the Oregon Coast in November is like that. The juice could squeeze people in either direction.

All the regulars lived in the park and had for years. Once you washed up there, you died there. They drove to work and walked to drink. It was a trailer park, but also a fishing camp named after an exterminated Indian tribe. There was no apparent plan to its layout, just a smattering of ancient campers, fifth wheels and fishing boats that served as domiciles. One was even an Airstream, colored green with moss and mold. All of them were on blocks. Most were tarped in blue. None of them would ever see the road or water again. There was a chicken coop nearby too, and hens sometimes wandered into the tavern or out on the street where they were occasionally flattened by semis carrying logs from the scorched clearcuts that marred the Coast Range every time you looked, if you looked.

Tom West was one person who looked at the clearcuts. He was a Mad Dog regular and semi-retired private detective who lived in the trailer park. Mysteriously, he wasn't defined by an OTA appearance. West hated clearcuts, those industrialized massacres also known as bullshit forest policy, because he loved Oregon. You can't claim to love Oregon if you think clearcuts are acceptable, but you keep your clearcut opinions to yourself at the Mad Dog. Some of the semi-regulars had a hand in their production. They were the ones who smelled like Sitka spruce and had various missing middle fingers, but still managed to get their point across when flipping someone off.

They never flipped off Tom West. They'd seen him in action when he was upset. He knew how to brace and slap.

But that was years ago. He didn't react much to anything anymore.

CHAPTER 3
"I LOOK LIKE LOU GRANT"

The telephone rang inside the Mad Dog, a real black, wall-mounted, rotary model that pealed like the Liberty Bell when someone dialed up the tavern, something that happened about as often as a German tourist walking in and ordering champagne. The telephone had a 50-foot coiled cord and a sticker for a Newport cab company that had gone out of business two decades before. The receiver had heft enough to kill someone in a fight, and in fact, had done exactly that, in a violent dispute over a choice on movie night (*Casablanca* versus *Lethal Weapon*. Bogart killed Gibson). Regulars said the telephone sounded a lot better after the murder, and beer washed away the blood and brain matter just fine.

Something else distinguished that telephone. Years back, a customer broke in after hours and hung himself with the cord. Threw it right over the massive spruce beam that buttressed the tavern and kicked the stool over with his one good leg. Paid for his beer and left a hundred dollar tip. No note.

The bartender answered the telephone. "Rose here," she said, not taking her eyes off *Perry Mason*. She'd worked there forever and lived above the joint in a studio apartment. No one knew her last name and no one ever asked. A Rose by any other name is still a Rose, and that was enough, although she didn't smell that sweet. A second later she tossed the receiver down the green undulating linoleum countertop. It collided with West's can of Rainier and stopped. The can leaned a bit but stayed upright. She was a pro.

"It's for you," said Rose.

West picked up the receiver, drained the rest of the Rainier, and said, "Hello."

"Is this Tom West, the private detective?"

"Yeah."

"My name is Matt Love and I live in Newport. I'm looking to hire someone to help me on a story."

"You a writer?"

"Something like that."

"Why not hire a researcher? Some college kid."

"I want a detective, not a researcher."

"How'd you find me?"

"The yellow pages. Your ad in a phonebook in Nye Beach. The phone was gone but the book was there."

"You're telling me that you looked in the Yellow Pages in a phone booth without a phone, but you probably have a smart phone."

"Yes."

"Is that some sort of writer thing?"

"I guess so."

"What do you write about?"

"Oregon."

"Oregon, that's it? Doesn't sound very lucrative."

"It isn't. Can we meet and talk?"

"Sure."

"When?"

"Tomorrow. I'll be at the Mad Dog. You know where it's at?"

"Yeah. I've been there. What time?"

"Just show up. I'll be there."

"What do you look like?"

"I look like Lou Grant from the *Mary Tyler Moore Show*."

It was West's first call for a private detective job in 15 years. He ordered another Rainier, glanced at *Perry Mason*, and tried to remember the name of his former investigation business. Something with a derivative of the word "ocean" in it. Oceanic? Oceanus? A few more Rainiers and he might remember it.

CHAPTER 4
THE TEACHER

It had been a prosperous day in the classroom at Newport High School where Love worked at his real job. Prosperity meant he had done something worthwhile and semi-clandestine to undermine the ongoing corporatization of the American public education system, a process also known as the Combine that came courtesy of politicians and billionaires who never sent their children to public schools and wanted to unleash market forces to improve public education and humanity. These same people thought privatization of everything solved all the world's problems, even the ones caused by privatization.

Besides writing books about Oregon that virtually no one ever read, Love taught three classes: journalism, photography and creative writing. Three, that was it. He didn't need the money and couldn't stand the faculty meetings. Two decades ago he'd hit a major score by pulling off the biggest jewelry heist in Oregon history. He buried the loot and waited for the statute of limitations of the crime to run out. He confessed in a book, but no one believed him. Creative nonfiction, they called it. From time to time, he dug up some of the jewelry and sold it cut-rate on eBay. He spent most of the money on his students and fashioned a mysterious and preposterous cover for himself as an "eccentric millionaire who teaches for pleasure." The kids loved it. They believed it, too. LOL! OMG! WTF!

Love was always done teaching by noon and always rambling down one of the local beaches with Sonny, his old, invalid husky, half an hour later. Weather conditions never mattered. Getting to the beach, one, two, three times a day with Sonny mattered. They both preferred visits in rain because that meant they wouldn't encounter another human being or see a kid playing on his phone with his back to the ocean.

Love was addicted to the rambling. It kept him sane and broke up romantic relationships. It was his recreation, fitness regimen, spirituality, writing studio, lesson planning machine, psychotherapy session and sex life all rolled into one primordial obsession.

It being Oregon, indulging his obsession never cost him a cent.

Yes, it had been a prosperous teaching day, particularly the gritty existential lesson in rain to his creative writing students. After driving home, Love collected Sonny into the truck and struck out to find adventure. What beach would they hit today? He relished having so many choices within a short distance. How people could live far from the ocean and the beach was beyond him. Of course, if everyone felt that way, there would have been three million people living on the Oregon Coast and that would have ruined everything. Thank rain. Thank monochrome.

In his 18 years of living at the Coast, Love had become Oregon's foremost chronicler of the state's unprecedented legacy of publicly–owned beaches. Actually, the only one, and self-appointed at that. He had researched dozens of obscure archives, interviewed hundreds of old timers, visited every local, state and federal coastal and beachfront park in Oregon, taken thousands of photographs, and written hundreds of thousands of words (772,333 so far) that appeared in newspapers, magazines, books, blogs and broadsheets, on posters, postcards, handbills and napkins. He'd also driven his green Ford truck all around the state to give one presentation after another on the subject—375,000 miles and counting. He'd gigged for a thousand Chamber of Commerce types in a generic Salem conference center; he'd gigged for two old ladies knitting in an unheated church in the dead of winter in Madras; he'd gigged for convicted murderers incarcerated in the Oregon State Penitentiary who would never see the ocean again.

It didn't matter. If a group asked him to speak about the sacrosanct great notion of Oregon's coastal beaches, Love was there, and he never failed to rile up an audience with his blazing passion for protecting the state's "great birthright," as former Governor Oswald West memorably described the 230 miles of ocean beaches along Oregon's 363 miles of coastline. West had written: "No local selfish interest should

be permitted, through politics or otherwise, to destroy or even impair this great birthright of our people." Love considered tattooing the sentiment on his chest, but teachers weren't supposed to do that kind of thing. It might smack of passion.

It was Oregon scripture, plain and simple. None of Love's high school students passed any of his classes unless they could recite the verse. They would remember it all their lives.

Oswald West recognized the great birthright for what it was back in 1913 with a 66-word piece of legislation that he wrote himself after riding his horse named Frank the Freak from Cannon Beach over Arch Cape and Neahkahnie Mountain and into Nehalem.

In a memoir he described the genesis and genius of his great notion, Oregon's perpetual greatest notion:

So I came up with a bright idea. And this was very much of a surprise for I have enjoyed but few such in a lifetime. I drafted a simple short bill declaring the seashore from the Washington line to the California line a public highway. I pointed out that thus we would come into miles and miles of highway 'without cost to the taxpayer.' The Legislature took the bait—hook, line, and sinker. Thus came public ownership of our beaches.

The bill, known as the Open Beaches Act, SB 22, became Oregon law and it read:

The shore of the Pacific Ocean, between ordinary high tide and extreme low tide, and from the Columbia River on the north to the Oregon and California State line on the south, excepting such portion or portions of such shore as may have heretofore been disposed of by the State, is hereby declared a public highway and shall forever remain open as such to the public.

It was the most utilitarian *and* ethereal use of 66 words in the history of American literature *and* politics. West's law changed Oregon forever. He helped create a unique and revered relationship between a state's citizenry and a specific natural resource unlike any other in the country. He established a birthright. When tourists visited Oregon's beaches, they simply could not believe they didn't have to pay anything to use them. Nothing. It was all free. It was a miracle to the visitors and they always shook their heads in disbelief.

Love met these visitors all the time, beachcombing the wrack lines, reading in the dunes, sitting on driftlogs, coming and going from the parking lots of waysides and parks. He sometimes struck up conversations with these perfect strangers and gave them a 60-second lesson on the great birthright. If thcy happened to come from Washington, and many of them did, it wasn't so much a lesson but a harangue disguised as a story. It went something like this:

I got a 99-dollar ticket at Cape Disappointment State Park in Washington for not paying ten dollars to walk on a publicly-owned beach for twenty minutes with my dog and take five photographs of three driftwood forts. The ranger was carrying a sidearm and wearing an armored vest over his military-style uniform. Here's what transpired:

I was on the beach for twenty minutes. That's it.

We have to maintain the facility by charging a fee.

Yes, you do for the users of the facilities. I went to the beach. That's not a facility.

You used the parking lot.

Well, you got me there.

Then the cop asked for my ID and I fished out my driver's license. He walked over to his truck, got on his radio or computer and checked me out without any probable cause whatsoever. What a drag of a job to ticket people who don't want to pay to recreate on a public beach. Or can't afford to. The ranger returned and handed me a ticket. He used my middle name as my last name. I corrected him. He replied:

Welcome to the park.

Some welcome. I won't be back. Ever. Washington sucks.

That sort of menacing confrontation never happened in Oregon. The mentality of the great birthright wouldn't allow it.

And now someone wanted to plunder the birthright, someone from Los Angeles, a developer. He was probably tan and wore shiny rings. He certainly owned three dozen fashionable umbrellas and wielded them like a dandy from a land where it never rains and rivers never flow but developers bribe politicians to steal water from places where they do.

CHAPTER 5
ONA BEACH

Sonny was riding shotgun with Love and twitching her nose at the old smell of the ocean. Love looked at her. Sixteen years of rambling together was coming to an end, but they weren't done yet. He wondered if he'd even know how to walk on a beach without her. He wondered if the writing would dry up.

Traffic was nonexistent and Love drove slowly, trying to decide where they would ramble today. Would it be the beach near his house with its fabulous covert spaces for cavorting and excellent limpet hunting? The one with deserted dunes at the state park with hungover surfers and waves crashing at the South Jetty? The one with a nameless creek that hosted a pair of bald eagles and the greatest driftwood fort in the history of the world? The one where the public access led inches away from the ornate dining room of an Oregon beer magnate and Love could wave "hello" as he walked past? The one where Steve Prefontaine trained as a kid without corporate sponsors? The one with the muddy cliffs and their embedded antediluvian shells and etched teenage equations of sweet horny math like $M + C = ♥$ or $JR + S = forever$?

No. It would be Ona Beach, where Beaver Creek meandered into the ocean, a smallish estuary where fresh and salt water collided in an eternal cycle that created the most fertile of spaces. The spaces were biological and metaphorical. There was poetry and science surfacing from every pool and riffle. They merged in metaphysical ways most high school English and science teachers could never imagine them merging in the classroom.

Love never tired of visiting Ona because it was never the same. Some unpredictable and magical encounter always transpired there. The area attracted an astonishing array of aquatic, avian and hominid life. Love met a gorgeous female jogger and they fell in love with each other for an hour. He saw a coho salmon riding a freshet up the creek to spawn. He witnessed Russian Old Believers practicing golf. He happened upon one of his students being baptized in the creek. He encountered an ingenious fountain made from kelp.

He talked to a marijuana magnate from Montana who brought his kids to Oregon to see the beach for the first time. He interviewed seven Asian men fishing in the surf during the Super Bowl. He helped build a collection of 21 driftwood forts. He espied a young man in obvious distress reading the Bible on a driftlog with his back to the ocean. He walked into a rainbow.

He played naked hide-and-seek in broad daylight in the dunes while drinking Cutty Sark. He collected hairy tritons, Oregon's official sea shell, by the dozens. He spooked a river otter in the willows. He held a conversation with a coyote, and received excellent advice. He watched a wedding where the minister failed to show up. He counseled a man out of committing suicide. He talked to a man in a witness protection program. He took his students on a field trip for absolutely no academic reason. He stared at the poetry of a roiling brown ocean. He snapped a million photographs of Sonny. He got his life in order on Ona Beach. He learned to write there.

Love never paid a cent for any of this and never would as long as Oregon remained Oregon and people fought to keep it Oregon, like they had in 1967 for the dry sand areas of the public beaches. In 1913 it had been entirely Oswald West saving the beaches from privatization;

in 1967, it had been an army. One of its Generals was a man named Tom McCall, Governor McCall. Love had written a million words on McCall's unprecedented accomplishments from 1967-75, and he knew he'd write a million more before he died. There wasn't any money in it, which made it all the more worth doing. To think McCall was a Republican! Maybe that was why Love wrote so much about him, because the inherent impossibility of writing about such a progressive Republican Governor of Oregon today made writing about McCall feel like writing historical pulp fantasy fan fiction, if there was such a genre.

The days of the Tom McCall Republicans in Oregon were long, long, gone and dead, entombed forever, and the state wasn't necessarily the better for it.

CHAPTER 6
RIPRAP

He parked the truck at Ona Beach and lifted Sonny out to the sand. The sky was like a jagged black and gray layer cake and showers blew lightly from south to north. They made their way along a trail through the dunes. Emerging onto the beach, Love witnessed a hundred Western gulls debating something in the estuary. The showers turned to rain, quit abruptly, allowing some furtive bolts of sunshine to reach the Earth.

It was the kind of weather that drove the meteorologists, weather bugs and real estate novelist-types mad. They wanted rain with numbered accumulations and clichéd descriptions. Love had stopped measuring rain with instruments and words long ago. It just was. He tried explaining this precise feeling in a book about rain, but no one seemed to get it except one intense woman with famous rain lines tattooed all over her body. They had tried to date, but she ate ham. It hadn't worked out.

Love and Sonny headed toward the creek and he planned one of their typical discursive excursions. This one would probably take an hour. Love had a lot to think through. Nothing less than the future of Oregon's publicly-owned beaches was at stake. There was a known unknown lurking out there and Love had to find out what it was and what to do about it.

In the last several weeks, conservation groups and ordinary citizens up and down the Coast had sent him one email after another alerting him to a shocking development: a shadowy holding company based in Southern California had been buying up all the undeveloped beachfront property along the Oregon Coast. These groups and citizens had been tipped off about the purchases by their friendly contacts in the real estate industry, mostly from the legion of agents struggling to make a living selling vacation homes where it rained 70 inches a year.

There was something else particularly suspicious about the purchases. The holding company was paying full market prices on every parcel, something totally unheard of in the coastal real estate market. Many of the parcels had been for sale for decades at ridiculously inflated prices. Potential buyers from outside the state were always scared away by Oregon's tough, nationally-renowned land use laws, particularly when it came to coastal development.

But the news that really triggered the conservationists' alarm was that Santa Monica Dreams, LLC had also purchased numerous beachfront mansions and motels that had been riprapped. Some coastal newspapers owned by actual Oregonians caught wind of the local angle but couldn't connect all the dots. Love made an initial cursory investigation and couldn't either. This was bigger than a story. It was quite possibly a criminal conspiracy, and for that he needed a detective.

If there was anything Love hated more than riprap, he couldn't think of it. Maybe Lars Larson, selfie sticks and people who kept their dogs on chains.

Riprap. It almost sounded Republican and was probably invented by one. A six-letter four-letter dirty word, the most profane word on the Oregon Coast: the ecologically unsound and downright ugly practice of placing large boulders on beaches to protect ill-conceived structures from collapsing into the ocean where they rightfully belonged.

Oregon's land use law allowed riprap on all beachfront dwellings, business or lots that were constructed or platted prior to 1977. After that year, if some fool built on sand near the ocean or bought a beach-front home and erosion threatened to disintegrate his property, they were not allowed to riprap. There was, however, no shortage of fools who failed to listen to the advice of the world's first wise land use planner, Jesus Christ. "Build on a rock," he said.

Unfortunately, the fools hired slick lawyers and hack geologists who always found loopholes in the law that ended up allowing riprap up and down the Oregon Coast where it should have never been allowed.

The issue was particularly raw with Love. He had recently gone to war with a rich couple from South Carolina who had purchased an abandoned and riprapped beachfront home built in 1948 that was mere inches above sea level. The couple planned to raze the structure, add more riprap, and build one of the insidious 5-2-2 mansions that littered the coast: 5,000-square feet for two people for two weeks out of the year. In the past few decades, this trend had become a disease that hol-lowed out formerly quaint beach villages.

Somehow, the couple secured approval from Oregon State Parks to dump more riprap, a lot more riprap, but what incensed Love was that they extended the riprap's footprint 150 feet westward toward the ocean, invading a publicly-owned beach, a beach that Love enjoyed very much and that once served as a spot for a very solid driftwood fort that Love used for wine-drinking, writing and seduction purposes.

One afternoon, Love was standing in front of the new riprap taking

photographs for yet another withering blog post, when he encountered a woman also taking photographs of it. He went up to her, assuming she was some local conservationist documenting the disgrace. He introduced himself.[1]

She was not a conservationist. She was the co-owner of the house and spoke giddily with an Australian accent about her imminent new mansion. They were breaking ground soon, she told Love.

Love was not a confrontational man by nature and had never used profanity in public when addressing someone he disagreed with on an issue.

"You and your husband are a fucking disgrace to Oregon!" said Love, his voice in crescendo.

It braced the woman. She nearly fell over.

"You have stolen public beach for your own fucking greed," roared Love.

---

1 The following confrontation between Love and the woman actually occurred in 2012. She hasn't been seen near the property again.

Goddamn, Love thought. *This feels good! I'm eating the rich just like the Motörhead heavy metal classic. I am Motörhead and heavy metal when it comes to protecting the Oregon Coast; the rich are merely Yanni.*

Love digested the woman and then promised a relentless cultural and political war against her, her husband and her mansion. He would call mocking and vitriolic attention to their desecration. He would enlist all the neighbors too, and the whole state of Oregon. They would hold event after event in front of the mansion, including a blockbuster one called the Oregon Coast Riprap Festival featuring live heavy metal music, fire dancers, naked beach fairies, hula hooping, effigies, obscene haikus about her and her husband's dismal sex life written in the sand, hectoring speeches delivered atop driftlogs, and rivers of cheap beer.

Love would never stop harassing them and they couldn't do a damn thing to stop him.

The woman backed away without another word. Love went home and lit up the phones and internet with the news of his encounter. Someone had messed with Oregon's beaches and they needed messing up in return.

While the South Carolina couple was in the midst of stealing the beach from all past, present and future Oregonians, Love submitted a blistering editorial and photographs to the *Oregonian.* He intended to catapult public opinion against this outrageous theft of public beach, *his public beach*, and the looming threat of more riprap on Oregon's beaches once the sea levels inevitably began to rise. There was no way they wouldn't print it.

The *Oregonian* wouldn't print it. The newspaper—if newspaper is the word—didn't care about anything important to Oregon anymore, least of all public beaches. Members of the editorial board used umbrellas, had never visited the beach, and couldn't write for shit. They didn't know anything of the state's unique history of conservation, and instead wanted to roll back everything progressive that made Oregon a place they wanted to move to in the first place. They thought University of Oregon football defined Oregon and sent triple the number of reporters to conference games than legislative sessions. They misspelled Port Orford in editorials about Curry County. They despised teachers and were shills for privatization. They had riprapped their minds and didn't know who Gary Snyder was. They'd never jumped naked into the ocean either, and that explained everything sorry and retrograde and desiccated about them.

Love was thinking about the emails and McCall. He wondered what Tom McCall would have done had he known about this apparent conspiracy. Half a century earlier, he had shown up, all six feet six inches of him, right on the sand, fighting against a beachfront motel owner to safeguard Oregon's public beaches, for Oregonians then and two centuries after, going maverick on his party, bucking all conventional political wisdom, on camera, wearing sunglasses, during a legislative session!

McCall's appearance in front of a motel on behalf of protecting Oregon's beaches from privatization was the most potent coded middle finger to the developer class in Oregon history. What politician would do that for Oregon's beaches anymore? Or for that matter, what writer would?

CHAPTER 7
THE BEACH BILL

Dear Reader:

We have come to the point in The Great Birthright where you need to learn the extraordinary story of how House Bill 1601, the Beach Bill, became law. The story borders on noir—one replete with shady developers, corrupt politicians, bribes and a scene in a seedy bar. It merits inclusion here at considerable length because of what will transpire later with the plot and characters. It also belongs because every Oregonian should know and promulgate it, lest Oregon become New Jersey or Malibu. Something else worth noting: even though this is a hybrid work of fiction, memoir, reportage, history and screed, the author has not invented a single fact, quote or primary source document relating to the subject of Oswald West's 1913 law, 1967 Beach Bill and the subsequent court cases. A full bibliography on the subject is at the end of this book, surely the only bibliography for a work of detective fiction in the annals of world literature.

The heroic 1967 legislative battle for control of Oregon's beaches began on a clam tide in the summer of 1966. An elderly couple and their nephew, Lawrence Bitte, were picnicking on the beach in front of the Surfsands Motel in Cannon Beach. They'd done the same thing innumerable times, as had countless other families. In a letter to then-Secretary of State Tom McCall (he would be elected governor later that fall), Bitte recounted the day:

Dear Mr. McCall:

Allow me to apologize for troubling you at a time when you are very busy; however, I feel that the item of my concern is serious enough to warrant your direct attention.

Tuesday morning, August 16, while visiting the Oregon coast near Haystack Rock (South Cannon Beach) I came upon an area of beach outlined with driftlogs and posted with signs claiming this particular section of beach was reserved for guests of the Surfsands Motel. Upon venturing into this "restricted" area on the assumption that the Oregon beaches were public property (under supervision of the state highway department), we were confronted by an employee of the motel who told us that the beach was owned by a Mr. Bill Hay and that we would have to leave. Proceeding next to the motel office, I was confronted by a lady at the desk who informed me that Mr. Bill Hay was not available. She also stated that Mr. Hay did own the beach down to mean high tide. I asked her how and when this ownership was acquired; and she said Mr. Hay won it in an Astoria court case. When questioned further on the details of the case, such as when it was heard, she refused to give me any more information; however, she did add that I wasn't the only one who had made such inquiries.

After reassuring me that Mr. Bill Hay did indeed own the beach to mean high tide, the lady at the desk asked me to leave. This request was reasonable because I had obviously obtained all of the information from the Surfsands Motel that was publicly accessible.

Upon observing this gaudy, modern Surfsands Motel, one notices that the natural bank which terminates the rest of the beach has been removed. The Surfsands Motel is built on a man-made earth fill extending seaward over what was previously sandy beach.

This brings several questions to mind:
1. *Does ownership of the beach property extend seaward to a point of mean high tide?*
2. *Does the owner of beach frontage have, with his title, the right to build earth fills out over previously sandy beaches?*
3. *Who issues building permits which allow a private structure to be built on a previously sandy beach beyond a point of natural terrain?*
4. *What legally constitutes a beach and can this term be widely interpreted?*

I am greatly disturbed by the situation at the Surfsands Motel, because I feel it establishes a precedent which will lead to the eventual defacing of all Oregon beaches and the take-over by commercial enterprises which profit from public use of the sandy areas of the beach. Since tempers are presently running high among those who are aware of the situation at the Surfsands Motel, would you please answer my questions at your earliest convenience?

Respectfully,
Lawrence F. Bitte

Bitte's letter, along with others complaining about similar boorish tactics by Hay, alarmed officials at the State Highway Department, the agency then in charge of state parks. They sent an investigator to Cannon Beach and the reports were confirmed.

Hay's actions constituted an outrageous affront to the people of Oregon. Even more shocking, they were potentially legal.

The pressing questions were: Who, in fact, owned and/or controlled the dry sands areas of the ocean beaches? What constituted the established boundary between public and private ownership? The wet sands portions were clearly covered in West's 1913 law, but what about the rest? Land titles had opaque phrases such as, "down to the meander or water line," but where was that in law?

To remedy any uncertainty, State Highway officials prepared two bills for the 1967 legislative session. Eventually they were merged into one, House Bill 1601, which gave the public control of the state's ocean beaches to roughly the 16-foot elevation mark above median high tide, where native vegetation began. This control meant zoning the dry sands areas as public recreation space and keeping private influence out—no hot dog stands, boardwalks, fences, barriers, gazebos or other ungodly structures that rich people, tourist business-types and unimaginative hominids prefer.

It was Governor McCall's first legislative session. He had defeated State Treasurer and Democrat Bob Straub in November. Democrats controlled the Senate and Eugene Potts was their leader. Republicans ran the lower chamber and Monte Montgomery was Speaker of the House. McCall had beaten Montgomery in the Republican primary and Montgomery loathed him. He thought McCall too slick and undeserving of the state's highest office—he hadn't paid his party dues, and worse, came from Portland television, a bully pulpit that garnered a thousand times more name recognition and media savvy than the noticeably untelegenic Montgomery could muster.

The bill landed in a House subcommittee chaired by Republican Representative Sidney Bazett, from Grants Pass, a timber town about as clearcut hick as they come in Oregon. Probably three quarters of Grants Pass residents had never seen the beach.

Bazett was a former comptroller for Columbia Pictures and Harry Cohn. After a career in Hollywood, he retired to Southern Oregon, and doubtless had seen the horror of Malibu for himself: fences that ran straight out into the ocean and established private beaches for moguls and movie stars. What else would drive Bazett to say things like, "The people of this state who can only afford a tank of gas and a picnic basket have the right to spend a day with their children on the beach without having to rent a motel room or pay a toll." He supported passage of the bill but his committee was dominated by a cabal of coastal Republicans, some with alleged financial interests in beachfront property, who didn't bother recusing themselves from the proceedings.

The cabal's lead henchman was Representative Paul Hanneman of Cloverdale, a dairy town as about as clearcut hick as they come in Oregon. Probably half of Cloverdale residents had never seen the beach.

Hanneman told one reporter the proposed legislation resembled the *Communist Manifesto* as if he'd read Marx and Engel's socialist beach classic. If he had, here's what he would have read:

> *A spectre is haunting Oregon Coast beaches—the spectre of privatization. All the powers of capitalism have entered into a secret lucrative alliance to materialize this spectre:*

*Chamber of Commerce lackeys and shady developers, mo-
tel owners and bankers, and the Benedict Arnolds of Oregon.*

HB 1601 was dead on arrival in the subcommittee when it landed
there for hearings in March. One beachfront property owner after another testified how the proposed law would harm them—take away
their private property without any compensation. Bill Hay, owner of
the Surfsands Motel, showed up and said of the log barriers he had
placed in the sand to mark his fictional private beach, "I was trying to
bring a little Hawaii and probably Florida to the beach."

Just where the hell did Hay think he was?

Hay also complained that the beach bonfires he built for his paying
guests were frequently visited by complete strangers just wandering
down the beach, with their beer and wine bottles. He didn't want the
rabble bothering his guests.

Someone forgot to tell Bill Hay that one of the greatest joys of Oregon's publicly-owned beaches is when complete strangers *do* wan-
der up to someone else's bonfire with their beer and wine bottles (or
joints) and start conversations with words or guitars.[2]

The only testimony in favor of HB 1601 came from a couple of state
officials, including the director of state parks. The cabal roasted them
alive.

2 Newport's Nye Beach is the best place on the Oregon Coast for this sort of con-
vergence. If you are extremely lucky during an inebriated late night or dawn visit
to this beach, you might encounter a convivial poet named Tim Sproul. Ask him
to recite one of his analog poems about the Oregon Coast. Demand "Fireball" or
"Newported."

Not a single Oregonian in favor of the legislation appeared to share stories of what the state's ocean beaches meant, not merely as property, but something much more meaningful.

They didn't appear because they didn't know about the hearings. Practically no one outside the subcommittee knew what was happening with the bill and this ignorance almost consigned the bill to the ashbin of Oregon history.

And then it all changed. It was called democracy, not the phony expensive one occasionally demonstrated today, but the real one, where an independent press informs the unknowing public of a grave threat to the public interest perpetrated by the government or private sector. Then the people (and some of their duly elected officials) get agitated, organized and primed. They start kicking ass for the public good and end up winning a great battle that improves the lives of their fellow citizens and all future generations. Yeah, remember that type of democracy in America? It was so long ago and so unlikely to occur today that you have to read about it in a quasi pulp fiction historical polemical class-warfare thriller.

With House Speaker Montgomery's blessing, Hanneman and company had the votes to murder HB 1601, but Sidney Bazett had dealt with the likes of Harry Cohn and wasn't going to be outmaneuvered by a bunch of Beaver State rubes and mountebanks. It was his damn subcommittee and he liked taking his family to the beach for free! It was a right in Oregon!

But Bazett needed help and a couple of breaks to wrest control of HB 1601 from men living at the Oregon Coast who virtually never visited the beach. These scoundrels wanted to establish a fiefdom for the propertied class who wouldn't allow serfs the right to surf wherever they damn well wanted to. They wanted to turn Oregon's beaches into everywhere else.

After writing his letter, Lawrence Bitte remained interested in the cause and followed the fate of HB 1601 from Portland, where he was a biochemistry student at the Oregon Medical School (now OHSU). In late April, Bitte grew nervous and impatient over the stalled status of the legislation. He called Bazett for an update only to learn that there was absolutely no public interest in supporting it. Bazett told him the bill was as good as gone unless Bitte convinced people to testify in Salem—like right now!

Bitte shared his frustration with friends on campus and someone suggested that for help he contact a professor of anatomy at the school, Dr. Bob Bacon. Bacon was highly respected and known to enjoy outdoor recreation and advocate for marine conservation. Bitte and Bacon met and the doctor took an immediate interest in the issue after he realized what was at stake. A transplant from the East Coast, Bacon had experienced the horror when the public doesn't own the beaches or have free, unfettered access to them. Bitte and Bacon decided to visit Salem to investigate, and testify if possible. At the last minute, Bitte couldn't attend because of a critical research assignment, so his wife, Diane, accompanied Bacon to the Capitol.

And that is where Dr. Bob Bacon stepped into Oregon history, literally.

Bacon didn't really know where the Capitol was. He didn't know if there was a hearing scheduled for the bill. After being told by a Capitol staffer that no HB 1601 about beaches existed, Bacon nosed around and discovered that Bazett's subcommittee was in session. In fact, the bill was being discussed—at that moment! This was its last hearing! The cabal was singing a funeral dirge with glee.

It was nearing lunchtime when Bacon and Diane poked their heads inside the hearing room and sat down in the back of the chamber. Bazett was out of delaying tactics and the cabal was poised to table the bill and pull a New Jersey on Oregon's beaches.

The gavel was coming down when Bazett noticed the two visitors. Instantly, the wily chairman seized upon a plan—a last ditch effort to rescue HB 1601 from the clutches of the cabal.

Bazett invited the visitors to return after lunch. When the subcommittee reconvened, Bazett, using his authority as chairman, summarily decreed the presence of two citizens indicated a public interest in the legislation and that more testimony should be gathered on the matter. Bazett invited Bacon to return to Salem for another hearing. The cabal was stunned but powerless to do anything about it. Montgomery was livid. A member of his party had turned apostate.

Bacon had four days to get something together, four days to galvanize an Oregon public oblivious to the colossal prize at stake. He was teaching a full load. He didn't know how to organize anything politically. He wasn't even all that political. He was a doctor, not a lobbyist! He didn't know the name of his state representative or senator. There were no environmental nonprofits to seek out for help.

So he, Lawrence Bitte and a few others, formed the Citizens to Save Oregon Beaches—the SOBs, as they came to be called. In four days, dozens of them returned to the next hearing and gave passionate testimony in support of the legacy of publicly-owned beaches and access to freely recreate upon them.

It was on. It would be impossible for the cabal to table HB 1601 now. Bazett's ploy had worked, temporarily. He didn't have the votes to send the bill to the floor, but more hearings were scheduled. He needed them packed. Bacon and the SOBs had to go to work.

They did.

The good doctor became the point man and cut an impressive figure with the public. He began making calls to everyone he knew who loved the beach. He hit the rubber chicken circuit and ate enough mashed potatoes and iceberg lettuce to last him a lifetime. He gave interview after interview. He went on radio shows. He called radio shows. He gave press conferences. He never missed a class. His superiors intimated that perhaps he should concentrate more on his profession, less

on politics. Bacon ignored them. He was working around the clock to rally people to save Oregon's beaches from privatization. His doctor told him to take it easy. Bacon ignored him, too.

Bacon joined up with a political pro named Ken Fitzgerald, who happened to live at the Oregon Coast. It was Fitzgerald's idea to caravan hundreds of coastal people to the Capitol and jam future hearings. This would lay waste to the phony charges the cabal would surely make that "outsiders" were meddling in coastal affairs. The SOBs countered that, "If you grew up in Oregon or have lived anywhere in the state for any amount of time, you are never an *outsider* to the Oregon Coast and its beaches. Beaches belong to everyone and their dogs."

The SOBs supplied Bazett with plenty of citizen interest to keep the bill alive, but he needed something more, much more. So he called up a friend, Matt Kramer, and Bazett did more than just talk. He leaked.

Matt Kramer was a veteran Associated Press journalist covering the Capitol beat. Many Oregon newspapers carried his dispatches on legislative matters, making him probably the most highly read government reporter across the state. Kramer was also a dedicated man of the beach, a driftwood fort builder, and frequently took his family camping at many of the coastal state parks. He made his own wine and wrote a book about outdoor cooking. Published in 1967, he probably wrote it while camping and drinking homemade wine near the beach!

Bazett gave Kramer tip after tip on the subcommittee's attempt to bury HB 1601 and urged him to start digging. Kramer did, and before it was all over he had written 50,000 words of hard news in three months about the Beach Bill, as he dubbed it, immortalized it, in the inverted pyramid style nearly extinct in contemporary newspapers. It was Kramer who first alerted Oregonians in print that something unprecedented and dire was happening in Salem although he never explicitly editorialized that. He didn't have to. He let the facts speak for themselves and the facts were screaming: *someone is trying to take your beaches!*

Matt Kramer's journalistic effort on behalf of protecting beaches from privatization was the greatest service an Oregon reporter has ever rendered to the Oregon people. He didn't send a single tweet. The only hashtag he ever used was #30 marked at the end of news stories he cranked out on a manual typewriter.

The single most important news story any Oregon reporter ever wrote was headlined "Beach Bill Revival Sought." It appeared May 5, 1967 in newspapers across the state and helped galvanize public support for the bill. The article, in part, read:

> *The legislators who side with property owners in the public-private fight over Oregon beaches believe they have the votes to win.*
>
> *A bill to ensure the public of the right to use accustomed beaches is in the House Highway Committee, where it met a 5-3 defeat the other day.*
>
> *Rep. Paul Hanneman, R-Cloverdale, said, "We have held a number of hearings, and heard extensive testimony, and I think the committee has made up its mind to keep the bill in committee," says Hanneman.*
>
> *There are 11 committee members, and Hanneman says at least six will vote to table the bill.*

Some property owners recently discovered they have title down to high tide line. Some fences and barricades have gone up on beaches the public has been using for years.

The bill would ensure the public the right to use the area between the high tide line and the vegetation line. The law already gives the public the right to the area seaward of the high tide line.

Hanneman and others believe the bill would take property from the owners without compensation.

"We can go two ways. We can compensate the owners, or we can have an interim committee study the matter in the next two years." Hanneman says.

Officials say they have received many messages in favor of the bill since the matter came to public attention.

The committee met Thursday, but the bill did not come up.
It will meet again next Tuesday. Rep. Sid Bazett, R-Grants
Pass, chairman of the committee says he believes pressure is
building for the committee to send the bill to the House.

Four days after Kramer's article appeared, State Treasurer Bob Straub held a press conference in his office. He owned a vacation home in Pacific City and liked walking his dog on Nestucca Spit. He loved Oregon's beaches. He would not see them desecrated.

Talking without a microphone in a lobby, Straub urged the subcommittee to send the Beach Bill to the floor. His warning was apocalyptic: "We're at a crossroads...to determine which way we go in Oregon." If the bill wasn't passed, Straub said, "You won't recognize the Oregon Coast four years from now."

Straub paused, for effect. "It will look like the East Coast or parts of California."

He'd just gone atomic on the subcommittee. Any mention of "California" was detonating the nuclear bomb. Oregonians loathed Californians, those macramé-wearing, tinsel town, freeway-loving, smog-filled, water hungry, Chablis-sipping Californians with their Malibu beaches fenced all the way out into the ocean! And no dogs allowed!

Straub then emptied the full atomic payload to the assembled reporters and cameramen. "If developers like the way development is occurring in California, I hope they do their development down there and don't try to do it in Oregon."

The day after Straub's press conference, Ancil Payne, General Manager of KGW Television in Portland, delivered an extraordinary on-air editorial. Bacon and Fitzgerald had visited Payne, briefed him on the crisis, and lit a beach bonfire under him.

The editorial opened silently with a drawing of a picket fence around Haystack Rock in Cannon Beach. Then Payne said:

All Oregonians should be deeply disturbed over the fact that we well may lose our rights to freely use the beaches of our Oregon Coast.

As every one of us who was born and schooled in Oregon knows, in 1913 Governor Oswald West declared that the beaches belong to the people, allowing us all the right to enjoy the ocean and the uncluttered sweep of the beaches for walking, picnicking, shell hunting, turning loose the kids and enjoying life.

There's a real threat now that this will happen—that fences and barriers will bar you and your children from the present easy access to the water and clutter up and divide the beaches, ruining the magnificent view and penning up the people.

This will happen unless the legislature takes positive action to prevent it.

This is the situation: sharp operators have recently discovered that Os West's law technically only set aside the beach between high and low tide marks for the people, although through the years the public has been free to utilize the dry sand areas above high tide mark. So a number of private beach front owners are laying title to the beach right down to the wet high tide mark and are planning to fence it off for their own private use.

There's a bill in the House Highway Committee which establishes state policy as being that the public has ownership to the vegetation line. This bill has only one purpose. It would not confiscate private property.

It would give the state an opportunity to establish in court which areas are private and which are public. It would also provide the public a means of compensating private owners for the use of portions of beaches which the public needs for access to its beaches.

Unfortunately, the House Highway Committee, under considerable pressure from vested interests, killed that simple bill. But now public pressure has forced the Committee to reconsider it at a hearing Thursday, May 11th, at one in the afternoon at the State Capitol in Salem.

There's talk about a compromise. There is no room for compromise in this simple bill, unless this is what you want your beaches to become.

There's a real and present danger that our children will not enjoy the beaches during their lifetimes as we and our fathers have during the last half century.

Do you want to save your beaches? You have but a few hours in which to act. The Highway Committee will meet in Salem

Thursday afternoon. Attend that meeting or at least let your legislators know by letter, telephone or telegram that you're angry about this and want House Bill 1601 passed with no compromise, no flimflam and no tricks.

Write, telegram, or call. Address your legislator, State Capitol, Salem, in favor of House Bill 1601—House Bill 1601— no compromise.

I'm Ancil Payne, General Manager of KGW Television. Thank you for your attention.

Payne got their attention all right. Oregonians who watched the editorial were shocked. *Our beaches are in jeopardy? What the hell is going on in Salem? There's a hearing tomorrow? Someone just asked me if I want to save Oregon's beaches?*

"No compromise," said Payne. He'd drawn the line in the sand.

In the next 24 hours, a record 35,000 pieces of mail besieged the Capitol. There were canvas bags full of telegrams, postcards and letters crowding the halls. There were thousands of telephone calls, too. All the messages said the same thing: *protect the great birthright!*

Pressure was mounting on the cabal and House Speaker Montgomery. They never saw it coming. Sometimes democracy can fall like a tank from the sky.

In three weeks the Beach Bill had journeyed from death rattle to cause célèbre of the 1967 legislative session. Everyone wanted a piece of the action and many wanted to water the action down. The cabal and

Montgomery went into action to save their asses from the ultimate political Californication.

At one point, Bacon and Bitte were summoned by Republican state representative Lee Johnson to the Thunderbird Lounge, a Portland dive among dives, to discuss a compromise and end the beach controversy. It was getting out of hand. House Republicans were getting blistered in the press. Montgomery had asked Johnson, a lawyer, to craft some cryptic language that diluted the intent of the Beach Bill, the result being an *improved* grab by beachfront property owners. It was a car salesman hustle, plain and greasy.

There was gin and whiskey and a dark room filled with cigarette smoke. Johnson insisted Bacon and the SOBs sign off on a version of the Beach Bill that established the state's control of the beaches to eight feet of elevation instead of 16. This is what the cabal and Montgomery offered. It meant privatization down to the ocean's edge on normal tides. *California here we come*!

Bacon and Bitte flatly refused; they knew that was a dead giveaway of holy public recreation space to private interests to develop or throw up the fences and NO TRESPASSING signs. They threatened Johnson with a ballot initiative that would take the issue directly to Oregon voters; it would win 10-1.

Johnson went red, exploded out of the booth, and roared, "We'll see who owns the beaches of Oregon!" He stiffed the SOBs for a $27 bar tab.

The representative was an Oregonian, elected by other Oregonians to serve Oregonians. He should have known who owns the beaches. But money does that sort of fool thing to rich people and their lackey politicians. They think it confers a special legitimacy on their decision-making that trumps everything else, most regularly human decency.

At another point, Bacon received a call from the wife of a coastal motel owner. She had overheard her husband saying that suitcases of cash from Reno- and San Francisco-based developer/motel interests were heading to Oregon for some "unofficial lobbying." She didn't favor the Beach Bill but bribery was crossing the line.

And at yet another point, Bacon thought he was being followed. He also felt his job was in jeopardy.

It was getting dirty, desperate, noir. It was getting capitalism.

Can you believe this is a true story and the author hasn't made up a single thing when it comes to the unfolding story of the Beach Bill? Well, it is, and he didn't. Are you sufficiently fired up by what Oregon citizens did almost 50 years ago to save the beaches for you to enjoy today at no cost? Are you doing anything to protect the great birthright today? Forwarding an email to your state legislator written by an undergrad from Iowa interning at a Portland environmental organization doesn't cut it. That's doing nothing. People have to *act*.

Bacon was barnstorming the rubber chicken circuit and doing radio shows. Bazett was leaking and running end runs, pissing off Montgomery, getting himself shunned by fellow party members. Kramer was cranking out inky oceans of copy. Straub was launching nuclear weapons and accusing House Republicans of selling out Oregon. The press was editorializing and cartooning hard. Citizens were angry and appalled and speaking out. Grandmothers, too! The heat was heating up in May 1967.

Still, the cabal and Montgomery wouldn't release HB 1601. They were like one collective hack Pharaoh wanting to keep something propertied that should never be property. They wouldn't let the bill go. But a great flood was rising over the cabal. It just needed a bit more water and a new metaphor. Make it a sports one.

Now it was time for Republican Governor Tom McCall to get in the game and punch the football across the goal line—against his own team!

To hit sandy paydirt McCall needed a gadget play to score, real grandstand, highlight-reel stuff.

McCall wrote Bazett a letter urging him to pass HB 1601 and protect the beaches from "crass commercialism." That was his feint, a fake handoff, a misdirection ploy.

The quarterback got the defense going one way and then rolled out the other way, pulling off the greatest trick play in Oregon political history. It was pure theater worthy of Hollywood, with a dash of science, right on the beach. In front of Bill Hay's motel! Hay probably saw the whole performance from one of his motel rooms, drinking a stiff cocktail because he could not believe his eyes.

A lot of other Oregonians saw it, too.

McCall decided he'd had enough of Montgomery and the cabal. He told Oregonians he was making a personal visit to the Oregon Coast and settling the matter of what constituted a beach and how much of the dry sands areas should be protected as public recreational space.

No, no, this wasn't about politics, McCall maintained. It was strictly science, and for that he would bring along nine experts from Oregon State University's School of Oceanography to define a beach with their instruments of measurement and objectivity. "We've got to evolve a formula," said McCall, something that would become "foolproof."

Naturally, the press was invited to join the scientific expedition. The agenda called for visits to Gleneden Beach, Rockaway and Seaside to measure beach elevations. The Governor would help, hold yardsticks and such, and peer through transits and theodolites. He'd talk transects and hold measuring tape with rational men in suits and walk on the sand. And of course there would be a final stop at Cannon Beach to check out the Surfsands Motel and its unsightly log barriers. The scientists wouldn't take any measurements there.

The expedition would take place Saturday when the subcommittee was in recess, perfect timing for the story and photos to land on every front page of every Sunday newspaper in the state. Oregonians would wake up on May 14, 1967 and read about a Republican Governor of Oregon going to the beach to help blast a bill protecting public beaches past an intransigent subcommittee run by his own party!

There was no precedent for this in Oregon politics, perhaps not even American politics. This was no underhanded scheme or deal finagled in a seedy bar. This was right out in the open, on the beach, where the whole state would see it.

The idea was nothing less than a public relations masterstroke. It didn't even rain that day. How could it? In fact, it was so sunny McCall had to wear Ray-Bans.

Bazett rode with McCall in a limousine. McCall was clad in black slacks, a black Pendleton shirt, black sport coat and black loafers. He practically looked like a senior member of the Velvet Underground!

But he wasn't preparing to play rock and roll; he was suited up to do what Lyndon Johnson had to do to help integrate the racist South when he was Senate Majority Leader, Vice President and President: roll right over members of his own party. Sometimes you need Machiavellian men and women like that for the greater democratic good. We desperately need one as President of the United States of America or at least one in every English department in every high school in the country.

At one of the stops, an aide for McCall brought out a sign that read, "Montgomery's Line." He staked it into the sand at eight feet in elevation, the level the Speaker and the cabal wanted as a compromise. It looked precariously close to the water and stood in stark contrast to other signs at 12 and 16-foot elevations. The photographers got it all, McCall's coded middle finger to Montgomery and compromise.

No compromise! Hey Monty, I just ripped you a new one and spiked the football on your political grave.

At Cannon Beach, McCall, the Governor in black, strode up to the Surfsands, and halted in front of the log barrier. He angled himself perfectly for the camera. He was calling out Hay even if he didn't say a word. The cameras clicked away. Photographers burned countless rolls of film. They knew what they were looking at. It went beyond news.

When the spectacle was over, Bazett and McCall sat on a log in front of the Surfsands. A photographer captured the moment. They had wry smiles on their faces; it was the look of victory. The Governor and

Hollywood exile had just teamed up with the press and Oregon people to rout the opposition—it took a little over three weeks.

You just know they had some scotch in the limo back to Salem and made profane and ribald toasts to Montgomery and the cabal.

Later that summer of 1967, the author of this book visited the very beach where McCall made his final stand in front of the Surfsands. He was three years old. He played in the sand with friends. Here's the proof. He's at the far left:

In reality, this moment captured on film is when this supposedly pulp historical detective work of 90-percent real-life environmental Marxist crime fiction truly begins. The author probably tracked home some of the same sand McCall, Bazett and Kramer walked upon.

Do you call that an anointment or something? Sure, call it that, an unwitting literary anointment with sand. When you get anointed, you follow through.

After McCall's stunt, the cabal and Montgomery caved. They were history. Their own renegade party members had crushed and humiliated them, and 48 years later they'd be lampooned as narrow-minded charlatans and traitors to Oregon in a book written and published by an Oregonian with some Surfsands history who would have never become a maverick writer and publisher had he not discovered Oregon's ocean beaches in their pristine condition when he was in his mid-30s, and come to ramble down them with his dogs some 10,000 times in 18 years.

Someone once said, "Winners get to write the history."

And publish it, too.

The subcommittee passed the Beach Bill up to the full House where it passed 57 to 3. The Senate passed it with a few amendments 30 to 0 and it returned to the House for a 36 to 20 victory. It was over; the people had won. All the coastal Republicans voted against the bill.

Axiom: never leave protecting the Oregon Coast to those who grew up and remained living on the Oregon Coast. Forgive them, for they know not what they have.

The Beach Bill passed the Oregon Legislature and was signed into law by Governor Tom McCall on July 7, 1967. Sidney Bazett handed him the pen.

The law read, in part:

> *Be It Enacted by the People of the State of Oregon:*
>
> *Section 1. The Legislative Assembly hereby declares it is the public policy of the State of Oregon to forever preserve and*

maintain the sovereignty of the state heretofore existing over the seashore and ocean beaches of the state from the Columbia River on the North to the Oregon-California line on the South so that the public may have the free and uninterrupted use thereof.

Section 2. (1) The Legislative Assembly recognizes that over the years the public has made frequent and uninterrupted use of lands abutting, adjacent and contiguous to the public highways and state recreation areas and recognizes, further, that where such use has been sufficient to create easements in the public through dedication, prescription, grant or otherwise, that it is in the public interest to protect and preserve such public easements as a permanent part of Oregon's recreational resources.

"Forever preserve" and "free and uninterrupted use thereof." That said it all. It still does.

When McCall signed the bill he quoted Oswald West: "No local selfish interest should be permitted, through politics or otherwise, to destroy or even impair this great birthright of our people."

CHAPTER 8
WHERE ARE THE HEROES?

Where are the Oregon heroes today? Love thought. *We don't have a Tom McCall, Matt Kramer, Bob Bacon, Sidney Bazett or Bob Straub around anymore to fight this next great battle for the soul of the Oregon Coast.*

Love sensed it was coming. Ever since the election of Ronald Reagan in 1980, much of the country had suffered from an ongoing political conspiracy to implant a virus to privatize, profitize, and corporatize everything. The virus had been successfully delivered to school custodians, school lunches, college loans, prisons, parks, forests, stadiums, torture. The virus was of such a malignant strain that it had weakened the resolve for community leaders and politicians to come out in favor of anything that proposed or even lauded elevating the larger public good over the smaller private interest. Love knew it was only a matter of time before the virus invaded Oregon and someone or some corporation would make a clandestine play to privatize the state's beaches in some form or another. And here, seemingly, the play had begun in the execrable figure of Ronald Ryan, the Los Angeles developer, something barely human that smelled very much like the ideological stool shat by Ronald Reagan.

Oregon seemed almost powerless to stop it. There were professional environmentalists who held meetings, sent out group emails, and worked social media. They called it activism. That probably wasn't going to cut it against big developer money with their hired geologists and lawyers. It never had.

Love took stock of what the righteous cause did have. It wasn't much of an arsenal, let alone a pantry. Mother Hubbard had more canned food and mixed metaphors in the cupboard than this shaky crew of two.

There was the self-published author who never sold any books and somehow fetishized the fact that Stendhal's 1822 nonfiction book called *On Love* sold 17 copies in 13 years. Love thought perhaps he should title his next book about Oregon *On Love* and see if he topped Stendhal's sales mark in the same period of time.

And then there was the sexless private detective who received calls at a coastal tavern in the middle of nowhere, lived in a trailer park, and collected VHS cop movies as a hobby. He was more Barnaby Jones than James Rockford.

Nevertheless.

They had something else, something powerful, something untapped: a million Oregonians living within a two-hour drive of the beach, virtually all of whom had recreated at the beach at least a dozen times in their lives and never paid for the privilege of doing so, which wasn't a privilege at all, it was a fucking right!

In the age of the Internet, hundreds of television channels, tablets, smart phones, smart watches, Corporate University of Oregon Football and an ever-expanding vast wasteland of bathroom-mirror narcissism, could Oregonians go once more into the breach to save Oregon's beaches? To become a new generation of SOBs? To have a heroic story to tell around a beach bonfire to a perfect weirdo stranger?

No, thought Love. And that made him want to hit the sauce *and* hit it hard. Or at least take Sonny on a long walk down the beach to dissipate the cynicism. The ocean was good for that.

CHAPTER 9
THE EX

After a soaked romp at Ona, Love drove the winding Bay Road to the Mad Dog, past the mudflats, oyster farms and derelict boatyards. Sonny rode shotgun in a special bed Love rigged up in the passenger seat. Buddy Guy played quietly on the cassette player. Love didn't listen to rock music anymore. Rock was dead. It was only the blues for Love these days, played exclusively on cassette tapes he bought for quarters at the local thrift store that helped save dogs and cats.

At one interesting curve on Bay Road, Love's thoughts drifted toward his ex-girlfriend. She loved rain, beaches and the Mad Dog; it was their infrequent Saturday afternoon hangout when she made the trip from Portland where she was studying to become a nurse.

They'd drink beer at the picnic table. She would smoke, laugh, flash him from above or below, he'd take Polaroids of her, and together they plotted the destruction of the cruel privatized world with their public love.

She had a heart that was "barefoot always" as Emily Dickinson put it, and this trait was the perfect counterpoise for Love, who never took his shoes and socks off at the beach.

They loved making driftwood forts together, too, and probably built more as couple than any other couple in Oregon history. Or that's what Love always told her when they were building the next one. She never failed to laugh at his embellishing. It made their small place on the Oregon Coast so much larger, infinite.

Love remembered their best day.

They were coming home from a day of scrounging the excellent thrift stores of Florence. They had both struck gold. He a dark blue corduroy jacket; she a crocheted bikini the colors of a rainbow.

Love was driving them in his truck north on Highway 101, a few miles south of Cape Perpetua, where there exist some of the simplest and finest beach accesses in the world.

They were talking about her future career in the healing arts. She'd healed him after a catastrophic breakup, just appeared out of nowhere on his birthday, and ripped him out of a severe depression. It was raining that day, of course.

The bright late afternoon light began to change, rapidly, like it had turned a sharp corner into a tunnel. They both noticed it and said something quiet to each other.

Gray was coming on, multitudes, relentless, gray, gray everywhere, enveloping, suffusing, blurred, creamy, woven, grooved, gelatinous, textured, tactile. You could puncture it with a stick. At least a dozen colors of gray piled upon one another to the horizon. Gauze, Vaseline, duct tape, pewter, slate. No contrast anywhere. Nothing but grain, like the long-lost grain captured on high speed film in the halcyon days before pixels.

Love drove without headlights because he didn't want to dilute the gray. It coated the car. For some reason, he turned on the windshield wipers. He found a wayside and pulled over. They were going to the beach.

They exited the truck without saying a word and started west. They found a trail toward the beach. They could barely see anything in front of them. She tripped on some driftwood and nearly fell to the sand. He heard her laugh but the noise dissipated into the sound of the incoming surf; the ocean was 100 feet away or maybe 1000.

"What's going on? I've never seen anything like this," she said.

"I don't know. Let's keep moving into it," said Love.

They cut through the gray, kept bearing west, assuming they'd find the ocean when they walked into it.

"I think we've walked into the grayest afternoon in the history of the Earth," said Love.

She came up to him and took his hand, squeezed it, then released. He looked at her, but couldn't really discern a face, just a vague countenance that deserved a painting, if any artist could imagine, let alone paint, grays like this. When they'd left Florence, she'd had brown hair, and was wearing a short blue skirt, black cowboy boots, and a white t-shirt. Now all of those colors congealed into a heretofore unseen shade of gray.

He touched her face, took her hand.

They hit water. A gray roller swept over their shoes. They pivoted north, broke into a trot, and talked almost exclusively of gray. She sprinted ahead a bit and he lost her in the muddle. He didn't bother calling out.

She reappeared seconds later and wasn't wearing the t-shirt or the boots. They embraced and she told him she'd found a crazy driftwood fort with cairns at the entrance. She laughed her goofy laugh and took his hand. She led the way to the fort. They went inside and down to the sand.

In most places in coastal America or Europe blessed with beaches, this kind of spontaneous magic could have never happened. But this was Oregon. The ability to access this magic at the drop of a t-shirt can do wonders for a soul. It's just waiting there.

She was also the best first reader of anything Love wrote and he felt a little lost without her advice.

It hadn't ended well and he hadn't talked to her in a year. It was all her fault and all his fault. The reasons didn't matter anymore because both of them were too stubborn to reflect upon them. Besides, they'd moved on to mediocrity after that, in love that is, and they both knew it. He wondered where she was living these days. He wondered if she had a Mad Dog in her life. They were pretty much disappeared in Portland.

Love pulled into the Mad Dog's graveled parking lot. Three men smoked in the cedar grove, the tavern's de facto smoke shack. It started to rain again and the chickens scattered for cover. Chet was making his way inside. It was two o'clock in the afternoon and everything was gray, the official color of the Oregon Coast.

CHAPTER 10
CORDUROY

Love entered the tavern. Three men sat at the bar. Two played Chinese checkers. Love wheeled to the right for a better look at the man watching TV.

Tom West *did* look exactly like Lou Grant. It was uncanny and oddly reassuring to Love. Lou Grant produced quality news at the television station and had a bottle of scotch stashed in his desk drawer. West was Lou Grant in the same rumpled shirt and short wide tie. He was the same height and had the same bald spot. He sat on a stool at the end of the bar watching an episode of *Mannix*. Empty cans of Rainier formed a semicircle around him.

Love walked up to him, introduced himself, and stuck out his hand. West sized him up, took a sip of beer, and extended his hand.

"You sure like corduroy," said West.

Love was dressed in dark brown cords, a red and black cowboy shirt, a knee-length tan corduroy coat and green corduroy Puma tennis shoes. It was the sort of outfit that made perfectly drunk strangers in Oregon Coast taverns come up to him and randomly ask:

> *Do you want some fresh trout?*
> *Are you the FBI agent who shot Randy Weaver at Ruby Ridge?*
> *Do you want to hear a story about Paul Newman?*
> *Are you Colin Farrell?*

Do you want to die?
Did you know Clark Gable had sex in here?
Did you know Lewis and Clark were really gay?
Do you know how drunk I really can get?
Are you in the rock zone?

"Yeah, it suits me," said Love. It did. It actually suited everyone. Love often thought if everyone wore corduroy all the time the world would be a much nicer place. Has anyone wearing corduroy ever murdered a watershed or another human being? Macramé clothing accessories were pretty much the same thing. Was there any correlation between the rise of corduroy and macramé as fashion in the 1970s and the precipitous decline of the American military industrial complex during the same era? There had to be.

"I used to wear corduroy all the time," said West. "Loved those three-piece suits."

Love wondered about West. Why does any man give up wearing corduroy? Something terrible must have happened.

Rose brought over a can of Rainier, cracked it open, and placed it on the bar in front of Love. He hadn't even ordered a beer, much less a Rainier.

"I charge $200 a day plus expenses," said West.

That amount and stipulation sounded vaguely familiar to Love. Where had he heard this…?

Of course! It was what Jim Rockford charged his clients on *The Rockford Files*, the greatest anti-hero detective show in the history of television.

Love took a drink of Rainier, fondly remembering that show and the sublimely indifferent days when no one talked about beer. There was beer and malt liquor. Now there was craft beer and craft malt liquor and interminable analysis of said beers.

Beer was beer in the Mad Dog. They had real problems there.

"That was Rockford's rate," said Love.

"Yeah. I loved that show," said West.

"Me too! Angel, the Firebird, Beth, Dennis, Rocky, Isaac Hayes, the trailer on the beach. That kickass theme song and the bluesy harmonica riffs throughout the show. The way he always held a woman's arm when she was crossing a street or going through a door."

Love stopped himself. He realized he was rhapsodizing, frothing, about a 40-year-old television series. He took another swig of Rainier to steady himself.

"The Rockford maneuver I called it," said West.

"I did too! Women love it," said Love.

"They do?"

West drained his Rainier and set the empty down slowly on the bar. It was looking like Fort Rainier on the counter.

Rose brought another one over. West cracked it.

"I hate the new detective shows on TV," said West. "All the high-tech computer bullshit and victims get sodomized, then decapitated. It's all too garish."

"I hear you. I haven't watched television in a decade. Garish. Good word."

"So what's the case?" said West.

"Have you ever heard of the Beach Bill? The law that protects Oregon's public beaches? "

"Yeah, I know a little something about it. I like walking on the beach."

That surprised Love. West seemed like a man who hadn't visited the beach in a century. It was hard to picture Lou Grant anywhere but snowy Minneapolis.

Rose put two more beers on the bar and Love launched into what he knew about Santa Monica Dreams, LLC and their bulk purchases of beachfront Oregon Coast property. The story lasted about five minutes. West didn't interrupt. When Love concluded he said, "Will you take the case, search out the real estate and land use angle? That's not really my forte."

"What is?" said West.

"More of the historical research and writing it up."

West picked up his Rainier, took a long swallow, and said, "So you think some rich prick from Los Angeles is trying to overthrow the very thing that makes Oregon one of the most special places in the world?"

"Yes. Something is up for sure."

For the first time in a decade, Tom West suddenly felt a sense of purpose. The last time was when he roughed up a tweaker outside a laundromat who was mistreating a dog. West confiscated the dog and took it to the animal shelter. He volunteered there for a spell, took in some strays until they could be adopted, but then West drifted away. No one knew why.

"I'll do the case for nothing," said West.

"You mean for free?" said Love.

"Yes."

"Why?"

"I'm Oswald West's grandson."

"You're what?" Love couldn't believe what he was hearing. He'd never met royalty before, let alone a Lou Grant doppelgänger swilling Rainier in front of him.

"I knew McCall, too," said West.

"What?"

"I partied with his kid Sam in Lincoln City and Salem when he was Governor. I was on acid at one of the family dinners and fed the dog under the table."

"You what? Acid? In Mahonia Hall? " said Love.

"Yeah. I also gave the Governor a ride in my VW bus one day after he finished golfing in Lincoln City. He helped me push start it, then we had a few scotches at his place in Road's End. I'll never forget what he said to me when he was pushing the VW. 'Tom, tell the kids how I'm a man of the people.'"

Love didn't know what to say, but he knew what to do. He announced to Rose that he was buying the house a round. No one in the Mad Dog moved a muscle. Rose didn't seem all that impressed with the gesture but she complied.

"I was also at Vortex for a couple of days. Walked around naked and ogled the hippie chicks," said West.

"You were at Vortex!" shouted Love.

Vortex 1: A Biodegradable Festival of Life was the notorious and free 1970 rock festival staged in a state park outside of Portland to forestall a potential riot between American Legionnaires and anti-war protesters. McCall had sanctioned it in the midst of a tough reelection bid. Vortex had the distinction of being the only state-sponsored rock festival in American history. It would always be the only one.

Yes, a Republican Governor supported a wild great notion and won a second term as a result. That's what used to happen in Oregon. Not anymore.

"I wrote a book about Vortex!" said Love.

"Really? What else do you write about?" said West.

"Rain. The Portland Trail Blazers' championship team. Driftwood forts. The Yaquina Bay Bridge. Oregon taverns."

"Rain? Why write about something depressing like that?"

"I was pretty much dragooned into it."

"Dragoon. Good word. I like it. You don't think rain is depressing?"

"No, not at all. I'm at my most creative then."

"I just drink more," said West as he downed another Rainier. He was quiet for a moment and then another can materialized out of thin air and in his hand in one graceful motion. Rose was that stealthy and that good.

"Look," said West. "I'd rather die than see our beaches stolen from us. It's not going to happen and I'm willing to do whatever it takes. Are you, Writer Man?"

West said it like it was an insult. Maybe it was.

"What do you mean?" said Love.

"You heard me. This is a pulp environmental historical crime regional revenge thriller right?" said West.

"Yes. Nominally."

"So there has to be blood, violence, clearcuts," said West.

"I'm not a violent person."

"What about existential violence?"

"I can probably do that. By the way, there has to be sex, right? This is pulp fiction! Dames, dolls and broads!" said Love.

"No, none of that. We're both past all that.

Love looked at West. Maybe Lou Grant was past it.

"Booze, then. Lots of booze," said Love.

West cracked another can of Rainier and raised it to Love. "Yeah, plenty of that. Cheap beer. Now show me what you've got."

"First, I have to ask you. Do you carry a gun?" said Love.

"Did Rockford carry a gun?"

"No, he hated them. But he had that .38 in the cookie jar for emergencies."

"That's where I keep mine," said West.

Love produced a sheaf of papers from his coat and set them on the bar. There were emails about the purchases, a few newspaper clippings, and information about the Santa Monica holding company.

West looked at him, then the papers, then he drank. "Give me a couple of days," said West.

"Where should we meet?" said Love.

"Where do you think?"

Love walked out of the Mad Dog. Rain had turned into drizzle. A new tint of gray had rolled in from the bay. There was a chicken on the hood of his truck.

CHAPTER 11
THE SEA GOD

Several days went by before Love made his way out to the Mad Dog tavern. It was a Saturday afternoon and Love drove the bay road in a slashing rain while Sonny snoozed beside him. Howlin Wolf played at low volume on cassette.

Love had pulled off a great week in the classroom and naturally it had something to do with the beach.

A new student had appeared in Creative Writing and Love had asked him where he had moved from.

The boy, a senior named Steve, said, "Nebraska."

"Nebraska!" Love had roared, the class roaring even louder. There had also been a few mumbled insults about corn.

Love had calmed them down and learned that Steve's mother had taken a new job as a nurse at Newport's hospital. Love asked him what he thought of the beaches. It was his stock question to every transfer.

"I haven't been yet. I've actually never seen the ocean. We just got in a few days ago and found our apartment," said Steve.

"You're joking," said Love.

"No. I'll probably go see it this weekend."

"You're going right now."

"Now? During class?"

"Call it a field trip."

"What about a permission slip?"

"Oswald West gives you permission. The ocean doesn't care."

Steve had had no response to that. He'd appeared sort of frightened and seemed to suddenly miss boring cornfields and worksheets.

Love had announced to the class Steve's obvious sickness and immediate remedy. His students nodded silently. They knew the drill. They were a trained army. In ten minutes they would rally at Nye Beach and execute Operation Great Birthright, as they had so many times before. Love also told them to bring wood and oil and a hackey sack. He'd round up Sonny for the indoctrination. Steve was going to see the ocean for the first time and experience his first beach bonfire—at nine in the morning.

Naturally, at the bonfire, a complete stranger had showed up, claimed alien abduction, and pulled out a harmonica to entertain the students.

Steve's cure was the highlight of Love's teaching life during the week. He experienced another one in his creative life as well. Actually, it was more of an epiphany.

He never saw it coming, which often happens when you visit the beach in moments of joy or distress. Anything can happen.

It started with two letters received on Wednesday afternoon from national publishers rejecting two different manuscripts about Oregon subjects. It was always the same reason—too regional. Whenever he read these rejections, Love swore he would never submit to a national publisher again, and then a year or so later, he would. He had admitted to himself that he wanted to reach a larger audience. He believed he had unique Oregon stories and an original voice that could do it. People in New York disagreed, or they didn't say anything at all.

After reading the second letter, Love loaded up Sonny in the truck for a visit to his local beach. It was the only way he could recover—to converse with the sea. Art was on his mind, as in: what does an artist do when he submits his art to the national artistic establishment in the hope of reaching a wider audience but the establishment consistently rejects his art? Does he quit? Does he retrench and keep trying? Does he take his art in a new direction hoping to please the establishment?

Does he embrace the role of maverick and put out his art his own way?

Love had been doing the maverick shtick a long time. He was tired of it, and damn near broke.

They took their familiar path to the beach. Love looked out to the ocean and noticed the tide was coming in fast, churning brown with lots of foam for good measure. He jogged out to the sand and pivoted north to the Yaquina Head Lighthouse.

But the lighthouse never came into view. Instead, Love beheld a series of some 50 sculptures, structures and altars of varying size and shape, all made from driftwood, burnt, barnacled or slimy smooth, all constructed and spaced within a 40-yard stretch of sand at the base of the cliff. As he approached, he noticed large words etched in the sand:

Sea God
Beware!!!
Dance!

Love moved closer to inspect. Over the years, he had walked into a lot of mysteries on Oregon's beaches, and enacted a few himself, but this was like nothing he had ever seen.

He gave a gentle kick to one of the driftwood pillars, expecting it to budge easily. It did not. It was buried three feet deep, as were most of the other sculptures. Everything was firmly anchored in the sand and the amount of work required astonished Love. He and Sonny had visited this very beach 12 hours earlier and there had been nothing but scattered wood.

A wave swept in and soaked Love's shoes. He didn't hear it washing ashore. In a half hour, the incoming tide would batter the installation and, in time, collapse it. Love realized that he might be the only person lucky enough to see this mystery. Someone didn't care if they reached a wider audience for whatever it was he was trying to do. Someone didn't care if another person saw his art. He made it because he felt like it. Or had to. Who had the time to do this? Who had this great notion to blow people's minds, or perhaps only his own?

Love called out to Sonny and started for home. He gave a silent thanks to the person or persons who made the art. He was never going to quit writing and publishing and he wanted to pattern his future projects on the metaphor provided by the Sea God. And what the hell, maybe it wasn't even a metaphor. Maybe it could serve as a political strategy in a fight to save the beaches—blow minds with mystery and ephemeral presence. Love knew with all his heart that if Oregon's beaches became even partially privatized, the mysteries he randomly encountered there that had brought him so much mystery achievement in his life, would soon vanish like the middle class in America had vanished, a process inaugurated with Ronald Reagan as President of the United Corporate States of America.

CHAPTER 12
RONALD RYAN

In the Mad Dog, Love sat near the window and looked out to the ancient RVs anchored at the edge of Yaquina River. Some were clearly never leaving unless a flood swept them away. One incongruous model particularly intrigued Love. It was the color of a human turd and sported white racing stripes and red Christmas lights. It was Conestoga wagon meets NASA spaceship circa 1970. Love asked a regular about the vehicle and discovered it was a Clark Cortez and built by a forklift manufacturer. Only 3,211 were ever made and Steve McQueen once owned one, quite possibly the sturdy derelict across the street from the Mad Dog. For some reason, Love drew inspiration from that possibility, as anyone would if they thought hard about Steve McQueen and all the supermodels he must have bedded in the Cortez.

Rain fell. Love read student essays about rain and edited them with invisible ink. West wasn't at the Mad Dog for the second afternoon in a row. Love had asked Rose his whereabouts but he might as well have asked her why Quentin Taratino's films met with critical favor or what was the atomic equation for Burgerville's secret sauce or who answered when someone dialed 867-5309 (a Newport number, incidentally).

The Mad Dog's medieval front door creaked open. Love turned and saw West enter the room. Rose opened a Rainer for West and sat it on the counter.

"Get me the Recipe too, stat," West barked.

Love sat down next to West at the bar. An episode of *The Equalizer* was playing, featuring Robert McCall, the mysterious English private detective, kicking some creep's ass with a vocabulary worthy of an Oxford scholar.

Rose put a chipped mason jar on the counter. It contained a purplish viscous liquid that seemed to congeal as Love watched it. West lifted the jar and swallowed the contents in one gulp. He grimaced.

"What in the name of God is that?" said Love.

"Blackberry brandy made by a couple of spinster sisters from Toledo."

"Let me guess, their last name is Baldwin."

West nodded and then took a swig of Rainier.

"So where have you been?" said Love.

"Los Angeles."

"Los Angeles?"

Love tried imagining Lou Grant walking around Los Angeles. He couldn't. It was like trying to imagine why poor white people vote Republican or Evangelical ministers ignore the precepts declaimed by Jesus in his Sermon on the Mount.

"What happened there?" said Love.

"I tracked down the holding company and went to the UCLA law library. I tailed the president of the company all over town for a couple of days. I bullshitted with some of his cronies at a country club. I had to drink Bud. It was hell."

"So what's going down?"

"It's a lot worse than we thought," said West. "It's a declaration of war on Oregon."

Rose brought over a couple more cans of Rainier. West didn't reach. Neither did Love.

West continued: "Santa Monica Dreams is run by a billionaire real estate developer. He's right up there with the Koch Brothers in terms of donating to Republican causes, except that he never gives to candidates. That's probably why nobody's heard of him."

"What does he fund?" said Love.

"Private property initiatives, challenging land use regulations, overthrowing environmental laws. He's constantly filing lawsuits all over the country."

"What's his name?"

"Ronald Ryan. God, I hate the name Ronald," said West. "The two shittiest things in recent American history are Ronald McDonald and Ronald Reagan."

West cracked the Rainier and took a sip. His hand trembled a bit. He said: "Ryan's Santa Monica Dreams set up a new foundation. It's called the Coastal Entrepreneur Institute. Its mission statement is, 'to promote private ownership and economic development of America's undeveloped coastal places.'"

"What the hell?" said Love.

"Oh, it gets better," said West. He pounded the Rainier and Rose had another one next to him in seconds, another act of legerdemain.

"Get this. Ryan chartered the foundation in Oregon. In Astoria, of all places. He bought a downtown historic building to class himself up with the natives and plans on setting up a high-profile office, kind of a think tank. Got a fucking tax break out of it, too. He's hired a slick PR man to run the show in Astoria and is going to launch the foundation in a couple of months with a massive media campaign, including television and radio ads targeted at Portland."

"A think tank in Astoria?"

Love knew the town well. He'd always wanted to move there, watch the mighty river, and write the great American high school teaching novel. He thought he had it in him, but obscure subjects like rain and driftwood forts always waylaid his ambition.

"You'll never guess who's the honorary chairman of the foundation's advisory board," said West.

"Who?"

"Antonin Scalia…who, by the way, has made a large purchase of coastal property near Gold Beach."

It hit Love in the face like a roundhouse left hook from Smokin' Joe Frazier or a medieval opinion written by US Supreme Court Justice Scalia, the Darth Vader of American jurisprudence, who believed literally in the Old Testament, but certainly not the parables in the New. It was the same scabrous Scalia who also declared corporations people, money the equivalent of free speech, and installed George W. Bush as unelected emperor of the United States of America.

"Fuck," said Love. "They're going to make a play to overturn the Beach Bill. I can't believe it."

"You got it. Scalia planted this demon seed 20 years ago. All he needed was a zealot with money like Ryan to water it," said West.

"How come people like Scalia and Cheney never die," said Love, "and someone like John Lennon gets killed?"

West didn't answer, just sat silently.

Love waited for a few seconds while looking at West. He was thinking he needed West to become Jake Gittes in *Chinatown* for this case. Matlock wasn't going to cut it.

But who would be his Faye Dunaway? She was gone. They had broken up.

West turned to him and said, "You're not going to ask me about my back story are you? Because this is probably the place in the book where a reader might be curious about how Oswald West's grandson ended up living 50 yards from the Mad Dog Tavern and drinking Rainier all day."

"I was thinking about it. I'm always curious how people end up in places like the Mad Dog," said Love.

"I take it you've read Dashiell Hammett," said West.

"Yes, everything he wrote," said Love.

"Then you'll know there was never any back story on the Continental Op. He just did what he did and the reader never knew his motivation, outside the code of being a trusted detective."

"That's true, but the reader does find out the back stories of Sam Spade and Nick Charles."

"Do I look like a Sam Spade or Nick Charles to you? Just get on with the sinister plot and vituperations against Republicans."

"Vituperations, good word," said Love.

West had a Rainier in his hand and held it aloft. How it got there was a cosmic mystery.

"Here's to good vocabulary in an ersatz Oregon-centric historical conservation-themed political payback thriller that no one's going to read!" said West.

"I'll drink to that," said Love, smiling, and he would have, if only he'd had a beer.

CHAPTER 13
MATT KRAMER

West and Love sat silently at the bar of the Mad Dog for half an hour. They nursed Rainiers. Outside, rain moved like a phalanx across the trailer park. Ronald Ryan was probably cheating at golf somewhere under the sun, thinking the grass around him was real.

Finally Love said, "What are we going to do?" There was desperation in his voice.

"You've got to get the word out," said West. "You want to be the next Matt Kramer, right? Well, here's your chance. One chance and we're going up against a lot more than a bunch of hick legislators. This is war."

It is true, thought Love. *Kramer is my hero. He changed the course of Oregon history with his journalism.*

All Love ever wanted from an Oregon writing life was something as simple and majestic as the Matt Kramer Memorial in Oswald West State Park, a stone and bronze tribute erected by the state after Kramer died from cancer in 1972. The plaque, which overlooked Short Sand Beach, easily the sexiest outdoor place in Oregon with all the surfers stripping and drinking beer around bonfires, reads:

> *The people of Oregon hereby express their gratitude to Matt Kramer of the Associated Press, whose clear and incisive newspaper articles were instrumental in gaining public support for passage of the 1967 Beach Bill. This*

landmark legislation guarantees forever the public's right to the free and uninterrupted use of one of Oregon's most popular recreation attractions, its ocean beaches.

Incisive! What a word! Who doesn't aspire to that aim as a writer? Fuck slant. Tell it straight. Love knew he'd prefer an accolade like the memorial over a Nobel Prize in Literature. It wasn't even close. Books may endure, but beaches are forever.[3]

"But there's no Matt Kramer if we lose," said West. "We have to win so we get to write the history."

---

3 Every high school and college student taking a journalism course at any Oregon institution should be required to visit the Memorial, lay hands on it, read the tribute aloud, and post images to social media as a requirement to pass the class.

MATT KRAMER

THE PEOPLE OF OREGON HEREBY EXPRESS THEIR
TO MATT KRAMER OF THE ASSOCIATED PRESS, WHOSE
AND INCISIVE NEWSPAPER ARTICLES WERE INSTRUMENT...
GAINING PUBLIC SUPPORT FOR PASSAGE OF THE 1967 B...
BILL, THIS LANDMARK LEGISLATION GUARANTEES FOREVE...
PUBLIC'S RIGHT TO THE FREE AND UNINTERRUPTED
... OF OREGON'S MOST POPULAR RECREATION, IT...
ITS OCEAN BEACHES.

OREGON STATE HIGHWAY CO...
1972

PEOPLE OF OREGON
ATT KRAMER OF TH
NCISIVE NEWSPA

"That journalism model is mostly dead," said Love. "No, it *is* dead."

"Then invent a new one. Or better yet, find an older one and refine it. Hit them where they'll never expect it. You're a maverick. Go maverick on them. Go vortex on them."

"We'll have to include social media," said Love.

West stood up abruptly and took his Rainier with him.. "Social media! What bullshit!" he said. "It would have never held our army together at Valley Forge or integrated America! It's a joke and owned by corporations gathering personal data for profit. You need real live troops!"

He was practically yelling now. He drained the Rainer in one swallow and sat down. Rose had another one in front of him in seconds. West didn't touch it.

"It's got to be part of the campaign," said Love. "There's no other choice."

"Then rethink how it's used."

"All of this is going to cost money."

"You've got the money."

"I do?"

"I read *Rose City Heist*. I checked you out. Sell some of the jewelry and get on with it."

"It's going to take a lot of time. I have to teach."

"Quit! Take a leave of absence. Sabbatical. That would be great for publicity."

That would *be great for publicity*, thought Love.

"It's time to get to work," said West.

"And what are you going to do now? Sit here and drink Rainiers?" said Love.

West shot Love the meanest, most withering look he'd ever seen on a human face. He would never doubt West's commitment again. He nodded a silent apology to him; West nodded a silent acceptance.

"Get me a poster about this quick and I'm going to put up 10,000 of them around Oregon," said West.

"Okay. What are we going to call ourselves?" said Love.

"What do you think? You sure aren't that smart for a book hustler," West said as he cracked open the Rainier and took a swig.

Love waited for a few seconds. It came to him.

"The SOBs," he said.

"Damn right," said West and he held out his Rainier until Love clanked it with his own. The collision made a dull noise, but it sounded like war in the Mad Dog.

CHAPTER 14
ALL HAIL SANDY
OREGON SOCIALISM!

It took three weeks for Love and West to piece together the SOBs. It wasn't really a formal activist organization, more like a contraption out of Willy Wonka's chocolate factory. They had only one goal—crush Ronald Ryan—but no concrete strategy to do so.

To begin, Love and West knew they had to spread the word, marshal a great Oregon army and prepare it for war.

Love didn't take a leave of absence from teaching. When he told his students what was going on, they all wanted to help. It was illegal, of course, enlisting them in a political cause while on the job, at taxpayer expense. Love did it anyway. If he got reprimanded or fired, it would be fantastic publicity.

The students relished being part of the conspiracy, acting out a hazy clandestine protest that, if successful, would bestow direct benefits upon them for the rest of their lives. Love got them to write haikus, limericks and sonnets on coastal postcards and vintage Snoopy stationery about protecting Oregon's beaches. The latter medium was an especially nice throwback move, felt Love. In the state capitol, years ago, he'd seen a letter on Snoopy stationery written to Governor Mc-Call in 1967 from an 11-year-old girl asking him to save Oregon's beaches.

When the students heard the story and saw a photograph of the letter, they dug into the stationery with madcap delight.[4]

May 8, 1967

Dear Governor McCall,
I am eleven years old. Ever since I was a baby I have gone to the beach. On weekends and in the summer we go. I am the third generation at our cabin in Tolovana Park. We have many good times. I hope you can save our beaches.

Sincerely,
Lisa Heath

---

4 Snoopy was an aspiring crime fiction author. In multiple strips, he sat on top of his doghouse with a typewriter and began his novel, "It was a dark and stormy night."

They wrote thousands of poems and the collection grew to the ceiling. When the time came, all of them would be mailed to state officials and legislators. They would bury the opposition with protest poetry.

Love slapped together a poster announcing the SOBs and the looming threat to the beaches. The message was emphatic, the look bold and Soviet right out of the Russian Revolution. He unloaded some of the jewelry and printed 10,000 posters, coasters and bumper stickers. West's job was to slap up the posters everywhere and distribute the coasters and bumper stickers in every dive bar and tavern on the Oregon Coast. *All Hail Sandy Oregon Socialism!* was the message and the aesthetic of the propaganda, with lots of clenched fists and driftwood clubs.

The revolution, however, would be fueled on Rainier, not vodka.

Love sent a letter outlining the issue, a real letter in a colored envelope, to every coastal county commissioner, statewide elected official and member of the legislature. He included a photo collage of the pantheon of Beach Bill heroes. He sent an editorial and press release to every media outlet, historical society, prominent political blogger and environmental organization in the state. He even submitted an editorial to the *Oregonian*, for all the good he thought that would do.

His ace in the hole, Love thought, would be senior citizens. They'd known the beaches all their lives. He sent a press release to every senior center and retirement facility in Oregon. He knew they'd announce it and put it in their newsletters. He imagined them getting very angry upon hearing the news. They all remembered McCall and the Beach Bill. They could still fight.

All these missives and releases were poised to hit at the same time. They would be coordinated with an onslaught of social media's usual suspects. Love also created a rudimentary website at www. SOBsofOregon.com. It was one paragraph, in black and white, summarizing the threat to Oregon's legacy of publicly-owned beaches, and listing all the social media opportunities. It told viewers to check the site regularly for updates and standby until urgent citizen action was required.

What that urgent citizen action might be, Love and West had no idea.

CHAPTER 15
THE PUBLIC ALERTED

The word went out all across Oregon through every conceivable channel possible, and all Love and West could do was wait. Would there be any reaction? Did anyone care about the great birthright? Was there one Oregon politician who gave a shit and would go to the sand for the dogs and the people?

They waited. Love went to the beach with Sonny, built driftwood forts, and then burned them to the sand in the hope of divining a holy message from the Sea God suggesting a heretofore unknown course of successful protest. With each burning, Love thought how much better the world would have turned out if Moses had divined his message from God via a burning driftwood fort on the Oregon Coast rather than a burning bush in a Mesopotamian desert.

Love burned away, but the message never arrived.

West drank.

Nothing happened.

The story exploded.

Every major print outlet in the state called or e-mailed Love about the story—every print outlet except the *Oregonian*. Portland and Eugene television stations were frantic for a booking. All the morning radio shows wanted an interview. About two dozen state legislators contacted him. Every one of Oregon's conservation organizations promised action. The Facebook "likes" went through the roof—a record in the history of Oregon activism. Instagram blew up #saveoregonbeaches and #Oregonsobs. There were tweets here and tweets there. Love's phone wouldn't stop ringing. He started receiving letters of support in the mail written neatly in ancient cursive.

The public was alerted! He had done Matt Kramer proud!

Now what?

CHAPTER 16
ALL TALK

Love watched the reaction unfold for weeks. It wasn't long before he realized something: it was all talk, all words. Ryan was going to win because of apathy. No one of their own volition had taken to the streets, let alone the sands. People had to be beaten and die to integrate America in the Civil Rights era. Facebook, text messaging and tweeting wouldn't have integrated America. It wasn't going to save the great birthright from rapine.

People had to put their bodies on the line, but were Oregonians capable of putting their bodies on the line for the most sacred greatest notion in Oregon?

Love didn't know. He did know there was no political leadership to rally Oregonians if this blast of publicity didn't work. The idea of Governor John Kitzhaber standing up to the likes of a Ronald Ryan in 2015 was a joke. Kitzhaber once riprapped his Neskowin vacation home and helped turn the village's beaches into the most inhospitable recreational space on the Oregon Coast. Riprap could kill people in Neskowin and everyone knew it. Imagine the ecological insanity that led to authorities placing life preservers near riprap so some grandmother or small child didn't drown on a beach because a sneaker wave trapped them against the boulders. This was the kind of insanity moneyed men like Ronald Ryan wanted more of on the Oregon Coast. They were the same deluded men who built golf courses in deserts. They hated nature as anything but a commodity. They thought a golf course in a desert was nature. They thought a private beach in Oregon was nature.[5]

---

5 John Kitzhaber resigned in disgrace as Oregon's governor on the very date the author wrote this chapter. See what happens to Oregon's governors when they riprap? It was also later reported by the *Oregonian* that, as governor, Kitzhaber pushed hard to have the Oregon State Parks Commission sell public coastal land in Bandon for a golf course development. The developer had contributed $10,000 to Kitzhaber's 2014 reelection campaign.

CHAPTER 17
THE SUMMONS

Love and West had gotten the word out and people reacted with passion. But it was mostly digital passion, and that barely qualified. There wasn't any proposal for legislative action. Love and West hadn't even bothered considering a step two. Maybe they assumed getting the word out and riling up the public was enough. It wasn't.

A couple of weeks later, Love and West were drinking Rainiers in the Mad Dog. The telephone rang behind the bar. Rose answered, barked her greeting. She listened for a second then handed the receiver toward Love and West. West reached out for it.

"No, it's not for you," said Rose. "It's for him." She looked bewildered.

"Me?" said Love.

Love took the receiver and brought it to his ear.

"Matt Love here."

"This is Ronald Ryan. We need to meet. I have a few things I'd like to discuss."

CHAPTER 18
"I CAN'T WAIT TO FUCKING CRUSH YOU."

The meeting was set for two in the afternoon. As usual, Love was early. He found a table near a large window in the lounge of the Inn at Spanish Head. The lounge afforded sweeping panoramic views of Siletz Bay and Salishan Spit to the south, Cascade Head to the north, and the limitless ocean to the west. It was located on the top floor of a hotel erected on a cliff, and undoubtedly many a developer had cut a deal there selling out Oregon's soul in one way or another.

It was pure bravado for Ryan to suggest they meet in this environmental monstrosity of gimcrack Mediterranean-themed luxury in Lincoln City.

Love ordered a double well gin and tonic from the bartender, took off his corduroy coat, and waited. He had brought along his journal but didn't feel in the mood to write. He was about to meet the richest person he'd ever met and all he could think about was something F. Scott Fitzgerald had a character say in *The Great Gatsby*: "The rich are very different from you and me."

Ten minutes later, a middle-aged man walked into the bar. He looked like a game show host, his hair slicked back like Gordon Gekko in *Wall Street*.

Ronald Ryan came over to Love's table holding a neon umbrella and sniffing a snifter of cognac. Love stood up. They shook hands and exchanged banal pleasantries. They both sat down. Ryan took a sip of his drink. Love hated the way he drank. It was Roman before the fall.

"I own this place now," he said. "I turned the top floor into a penthouse. I've moved in to oversee the foundation's effort."

It was a total non sequitur but Love would follow.

"Naturally," said Love. "It's only right that someone who wants to murder the Oregon Coast would own it."

Ryan didn't flinch. He swished his cognac back and forth like the way you swished your cognac mattered in life.

"You've made a lot noise," said Ryan, "but it's not going to amount to anything. We're ready to litigate up and down the Coast, challenging the constitutionality of the Beach Bill in a dozen places. Climate change is going to wreak havoc with the shoreline here in the next 25 years and I will be ready. We've got a sympathetic Supreme Court now. I predict three years before they overturn it."

"I don't understand. Why Oregon? Why the property rights zealotry here? There's no money to be made on the Oregon Coast. It rains all the time," said Love.

"It's not about money. It's about the principle of making money. That someone who owns private property is free to develop as he sees fit without interference from the government. That's what built this country," said Ryan nonchalantly.

Love almost responded by saying, "Actually slave labor, watershed rapine and genocide did," but he held his tongue. Why bother with a history lesson?

Ryan continued: "Do you know that the original words of the *Declaration of Independence* read 'life, liberty and the pursuit of property,' not happiness?"

"I did. Even the slaveholders back then thought it too crass," said Love.

"They should have left it in. Happiness is private property," said Ryan.

He took another sip of his cognac. "I hate socialism, stringing up a hammock for people who don't want to work. I'm out to cut down the hammocks."

Love thought, *who says shit like this when so many American children and veterans of Iraq and Afghanistan live in poverty?* For one second, Love considered smashing his gin and tonic glass right through Ryan's left eye.

His mother, a master grade school teacher of 34 years who never missed a day of class, would not approve. But even she was getting angry of late about the selfishness of people, Republicans in particular. Recently, he had heard her swear for the first time. "Damn it...don't these people care about the poor!"

"No, they don't," Love had replied. "They want to make them poorer and then blame them for their own poverty."

Love thought about launching into a discourse about all the hardworking poor parents of the students he taught and the tangible benefits of modern socialism in Oregon, like Silver Falls State Park, Timberline Lodge, the Yaquina Bay Bridge, and so forth, but he stopped. Ryan was swinging in his own hammock of ideological fantasy, the same one Ronald Reagan had woven so expertly from outright lies and thin air 35 years before. Ronald Reagan had ruined the American dream for millions of hopeful Americans and then accused them of hammock-swinging on the public dime.

What was the point? Convincing Ryan of American reality would be like trying to convince a 1965 George Wallace that miscegenation was sexy. Besides, it wasn't a teaching moment; this was politics!

Love sipped his gin and tonic. It was watered down. Ryan even cut his booze.

Ryan pointed to the journal. "So you're a writer. A self-published one, I've learned," he said. "Who won't sell his books on Amazon. An idealist."

"Yes, I write about Oregon history."

Love was formulating a couple dozen rejoinders to Ryan's remarks, but knew he wouldn't say them. Sitting three feet from an utterly soulless human being wearing sunglasses indoors, Love almost felt sorry for Ryan. He wished West had come along. West wouldn't have held back.

"I checked you out, picked up a few of the books," said Ryan. "I didn't get the rain one at all and what's with the driftwood forts book?"

"You've never built one, I take it," said Love.

"No. What's the point?"

How could Love possibly explain the innumerable benefits of building driftwood forts on the Oregon Coast to a spiritually bankrupt rich man like Ronald Ryan? How could he explain that driftwood fort building represented a magically tactile collaboration between people and nature that provided recreation, community, shelter, a cyclical understanding of the impermanence of existence, and inspired a fortitude for life and love?

"You should try it," said Love. "It might change your life."

Ryan stared at him vacantly. You could tell he didn't listen to people very often. It glassed him over.

"But the Vortex story is wild," said Ryan. "A Republican Governor, too. McCall no less. The days of Tom McCall are long gone in this state."

"That is true," said Love. "But we've got the public. All you have is money."

"You're not naïve enough to believe we live in a democracy are you?" said Ryan in monotone. The word democracy was hard for him to say.

"I'm counting on it."

"Look," said Ryan. "Let's get to it. I've got a check for a million dollars for a two-year film option on the Vortex book. I've got Sean Penn interested in the part of McCall."

"What? Sean Penn?" said Love.

"I can get any movie made I want with any hack liberal actor I need. I know everybody. Are you interested?"

Ryan produced the check. He waved it gently in the air like a green surrender flag.

"Done," said Love.

He reached for the check, snatched it from Ryan's grasp, and folded it into his wallet with one graceful motion that visibly surprised Ryan. He obviously hadn't expected Love to take it.

"You thought I wouldn't do it?" said Love. "Fuck that. My father was a minister in Texas and taught me his philosophy of taking money from the dark side to do good work. He said, 'Satan's had it long enough.'"

Love was on a roll. "I'll spend every cent of your money to defeat you, Ryan. I will relish the irony of that. So will the press. And you better not cancel this fucking check. It's all about bucks and the rest is conversation, right?"

Love relished quoting classic *Wall Street* lines on capitalism in his pursuit of Oregon socialism.

Ryan lapped the last of his cognac. He was silent.

Love changed his mind about not embracing the teaching moment, because clearly one was staring him in the face. They don't often come around for insulated men like Ronald Ryan.

He knocked back the rest of the gin and tonic. Teacher moments don't come fueled on shitty gin very often, either. Maybe the world would be a better place if they did.

"You know what President Lyndon Johnson said to Senator Richard Russell when Russell was blocking the integration of America? He said, 'I'm going to roll right over you.' He did."

Ryan pulsed with anger. "Roll over me? With what? Protests? People? That's a joke. You made some noise and it will fade away. And it will be exactly the same as gun control after Newtown."

Newtown was a good historical punch thrown by Ryan. Love took it without flinching. His jaw never moved.

"I'm going to come at you with things that you've never seen before or even imagined," said Love. "I'll come at you deep from the reservoir of Oregon's heart...hey that's pretty good...reservoir of Oregon's heart....I'm going to use that when I write the book on this and I will write it because the winners write the history, Ryan. I can't wait to fucking crush you."

Ryan stood up quickly from the table. "We'll see who owns the beaches of Oregon!" he roared and strode out of the bar. He left his umbrella behind. Love snapped it in two across his knees and sat there, looking out the window. A Western gull appeared, inches from the glass. It winked. It took a shit. He loathed Ryan, too.

CHAPTER 19
THERE WILL BE FLESH
AND SAND

West waited outside the Inn at Spanish Head in his late model sedan—a 1979 Chrysler LeBaron coupe, the luxury V-8-powered vehicle hawked by Ricardo Montalbán that featured a red Corinthian leather interior and simulated wood trim. West was the car's original owner and at various times had lived out of the sedan and traversed the Alaska Highway in it. It had never been garaged or washed in 37 years on the Oregon Coast and was streaked with mold and moss and sported a small forest of conifer seedlings growing from its various crevices. Call it a nurse car instead of a nurse log. The LeBaron had formerly been tan, but now was colored a combination of green and gray that only existed on the Oregon Coast.

Black clouds began rolling in from the ocean and West welcomed them. It was a good omen for kicking tanned ass.

West felt some music might help him pleasurably pass the time. An 8-track tape of Cheap Trick's *Live at Budokan* was stuck permanently inside the player. Every other year West punched it up. "Dream Police" was his favorite rock song of all time, but rock was dead now, so why bother? Instead, West dialed up some cornpone country station on AM radio. He heard a singer croon about his woman dumping him and leaving nothing to eat in the trailer except a cold can of chili. *What the hell did that Rhinestone Cowboy know?* thought West. He always shredded Swiss cheese, garlic and onions into his can of chili and doused it with cumin and whiskey. He also always heated it up. No man should eat cold chili from a can because a woman dumped him. A dog dying perhaps, but never a woman.

A long time ago, West had been a master chef and a game warden. Then, the terrible thing happened. A woman, an elementary teacher he met through a colleague. She had loved beaches and noir films. West had ruined the relationship with his reclusive moods and resistance to vacation anywhere outside of Lincoln County. She left him, and a slow float down the Rainier River ensued with an occasional crash on the levee of cherry schnapps. He had trouble holding jobs and finally decamped at the Mad Dog, living on Social Security, bottle returns, and the odd detective gig that typically amounted to observing someone faking a disability claim.

Ryan exited the Inn and slithered over to his Hummer. He burned rubber out of the parking lot and headed south down Highway 101. West followed him and was mildly surprised to see Ryan hadn't noticed the lengthy warning keyed along the driver's side of the Hummer: OREGON'S COMING FOR YOU, ASSHOLE!

Terse is always better when you are ready to get down to it.

West tailed Ryan into the Salishan Resort and watched him saunter into the lobby. He parked the LeBaron and followed Ryan. He wasn't really sure what he was going to do when he faced Ryan. Maybe he would throw a drink in his face or maybe he would school him on Tom McCall. It would play out like an existential eddy in the estuary of life.

Ryan sat alone at a table, his phone resting near a full glass of Chardonnay, a gutless California brand. West sat down at the table, picked up the phone, one of the fancy new Apple gadgets, and dropped it into the glass, where it sank elegantly to the bottom.

It happened so fast that Ryan couldn't react. It was practically a ballet movement by West, if vandalizing a smartphone can be said to resemble an artistic form. Yes, it is. More of us should vandalize them and rhapsodize about it.

"I'm calling the cops," said Ryan.

West nodded toward the glass. "I guess not," he said.

"Who are you? What do you want?" said Ryan. He appeared confused.

"Oregon is coming for you," said West.

"What's that supposed to mean?" said Ryan.

"That we are going to kick your ass—and—"

West stopped. He was feeling something. Strange. Alien. What was it?

He waited for the answer. Whatever it was, it felt good. He was the Grinch growing a heart. He was Scrooge on Christmas morning.

It came to him with the crispness of Rainier sipped around a campfire. Passion. It was passion for something.

Holy shit! West thought. *I've got a passion again. Saving Oregon's beaches!*

"You know, I don't like you," said West. "You look like Ted Baxter on the *Mary Tyler Moore Show* and act like the character he played on *Caddyshack*."

West was on a roll. Ryan was speechless. What was this man talking about?

"Just leave Oregon and go back to Los Angeles," said West.

"I live in Oregon now," said Ryan. "I've got a plan for the beaches. That's what this is all about. You and the socialist teacher."

"You have no idea where you live. We're going to teach you. There will be flesh," said West.

Hey, thought West, *that sounded pretty good, pretty hard boiled, pretty classic detective fiction. There will be flesh! And sand! Sounds very Tyrone Power. I'll be sure to mention it to Love. He could use the help, seeing that no one publishes him except himself.*

"I'm getting security," said Ryan.

Ryan got up and dashed out of the bar.

West was gone when security arrived. Before leaving the resort, he carved another sentence on the Hummer. It gleamed beautifully in the light after he pissed on it: "THE GREAT BIRTHRIGHT LIVES!"

An hour later, Ryan read the scratches. He was livid. He wanted to call a lackey and scream.

But his phone was dead, deader than every soul of every Republican Senator from the 11 states of the former Confederacy.

Ryan got into the Hummer, muttering to himself: "Great birthright? What's that? Who are these people? These Oregonians?"

CHAPTER 20
A GREAT NOTION

Love got up from the table and walked slowly to the bar. He asked the bartender for a Rainier.

"What's a Rainier?" he said.

"I'll take a double Cutty Sark on the rocks," said Love.

The drink materialized a few minutes later. Love took a sip and then looked south out the window to Salishan Spit and all the vacation homes built on sand and riprapped to death. Without the Beach Bill to forestall this type of ill-conceived beachfront development, the entire Oregon Coast would have ended up like this.

It was a good ugly reminder to all Oregonians of what might have been or might yet be.

Love took another sip of Cutty. A couple Western gulls rode the thermals past the window. Below, he saw three women jogging down the beach with five dogs, a couple of driftwood forts nestled well above the wrack line, and an elderly couple hunting agates. He saw the best of what Oregon had to offer.

What would it take to galvanize Oregonians? To get them off their asses? To fight Ronald Ryan to the death?

Love had a notion, possibly a great one. *Maybe we don't need an Os-*

wald West or Tom McCall this time. This type of politician simply can't exist today, so why bother looking for her? It's a complete waste of time. There is no time.

A couple more tastes of Cutty and the notion grew into a concrete idea: *We the People of Oregon would do it! All hail the Oregon People and their running beach dogs!*

And just like that, this ostensibly pulp historical detective novel became quasi historical inspirational utopian egalitarian fantasy fiction—an entirely new literary genre!

CHAPTER 21
THE PEOPLE!

It had to be the people. They would supply urgent citizen action equal to the heroic effort to pass the Beach Bill. No, they would top it!

Love sensed there was only one strategy to employ. He had to venture boldly, outrageously, to win the war. He had to free what the Puritans and Evangelicals had imprisoned for centuries. There was no other way. Nothing could be held in reserve.

Love needed sex and sex and sex. He would sell the sizzle, not the steak.

He would create fun-loving spectacle and ridiculous mystery, not campaign drudgery. To do that, he would go deep into the circus play-book of Oregon's most famous impresario, Ken Kesey, the originator of Keep Oregon Weird. You were either on the beach or you were not.

Yes, it was true that the Oregon Coast was not generally regarded as a renowned kingdom of bare skin and *From Here to Eternity*-type moments. It rained too much and the water was too cold. In fact, Love had never seen a woman in a bikini on the beach in 18 years of living there.

So what? Bikinis were Hollywood and *Sports Illustrated* and tanned clichés when it came to the idea of beach sexiness. This was the Oregon Coast and all hail the ineffable beauty of pallor!

There was something unique about the sensuality of the Oregon Coast,

if you were intuitive enough to grasp it. Gray was sexy. You got to make fires and build forts with no one around to dissuade you from acting out beach bonfire and driftwood fort fantasies. You didn't have to travel to places where corporations enslaved the sun and monkeys for banal new age insights. You didn't have to rent a room. You didn't have to talk to anyone. The sand wasn't trucked in.

Love had to get weird on Southern California and their twisted version of beachfront property and beachfront recreation. He had to remind people of Oregon's long unparalleled history of weird that boasted the proud lineage of Kesey and the Pranksters, Vortex I: A Biodegradable Festival of Life, Bill Walton living in a commune, Steve Prefontaine running wild in the Coos Bay dunes, and Bud Clark and the Mayor's Ball. He had to get so weird that Santa Monica Dreams, LLC and Ronald Ryan would never want anything to do with the Oregon Coast again. It would be a terrible investment for them. Super sexy mysterious weird would win the war! Going super weird also didn't cost a cent.

To get weird, to go Beaver State-medieval-Kesey on Ryan's ass, meant Love needed sexy men and women, and everything in between and under the clouds, unnerving the grasping wastrels of the land in as many Freudian and Dada and PT Barnum and Martin Luther King Jr. ways as possible.

He needed sexy t-shirts and shorts with a sexy SOBs logo—*make sure a bucktoothed beaver is on them!*

He needed grandmothers and grandfathers—*with nothing on!*

He needed strippers pole dancing inside driftwood forts. *That would go viral!*

He needed thousands of dogs. *Release the hounds!*

He needed thousands of dogs that could help build driftwood forts. *Fetch me that stick for Oregon!*

He needed every former Oregon high school cross country runner doing their best Steve Prefontaine. *Stop Pre!*

He needed the lunatic open carry advocates slinging their automatic weapons around their shoulders—*bare-assed*!

He needed Oregon celebrities. *Were there any? Did Storm Large count? What about the Portlandia people?*

He needed Oregon rock and roll resurrected and turned up to 11. *Indie rock wasn't going to cut it!*

He needed New Age-types with their crystals and potions and flowing vestments. *Bring wood and oil!*

He needed the animal kingdom. He needed whales delivering a splashing show at Depoe Bay and sea lions staging a crawl-in on beaches all along the Oregon Coast. They would ally with the species that nearly rendered them extinct. *It was their beach, too!*

He needed a Burning Fort Man on Short Sands Beach. Build a 100-foot tall fort and light it up. *They would all collectively hex Ryan.*

He needed it to rain and never stop raining. *It would drown all the Southern Californians!*

He needed Latino families—the new face of Oregon. Twenty years ago, he never saw Latinos recreating on the beaches. Now he saw them all the time. *It was their birthright, too!*

He needed the return of the Sea God. *How does one summon a god?*

He needed professional wrestlers and chamber musicians. *Put on a show together!*

He needed children with painted faces dancing and screaming around beach bonfires. *Think* Lord of the Flies *without the bullying.*

He needed majestic sandcastles with potent political content. *Build sandy Mt. Rushmores of West, McCall, Bacon, Kramer everywhere along the Oregon Coast. Build middle fingers flipping off beachfront mansions!*

He needed a million cairns on the beach. *Create some druidic mystery.*

He needed naked bike riders and naked horse riders. *Would they come like Theoden's cavalry in* Lord of the Rings?

He needed every surfer in Oregon. *You can either surf or fight!*

He needed people to embrace the Call of the Wild and the Spell of the Sensuous. *Get off your asses and phones!*

He needed the weird to turn pro and go where no weird had gone before.

My God! He needed OTA crews naked on the beach—*drinking Rainiers!*

It was West's idea to recruit the OTAs. These people may have spent a lot of time drinking in coastal taverns, but they'd also spent a lot of time on beaches with their dogs. They could become a formidable army, West said, but he also knew he'd get exactly one collective, herculean and unprecedented freak show political use out of them, and then they'd disband. West told Love he'd ripped off the strategy from Hunter S. Thompson's campaign to become Aspen's mayor in 1970. Thompson had mustered the city's various freaks and tavern denizens to turn out and vote for him, knowing he had only one chance to win.

Thompson lost, but then again, he didn't have the beach nearby or bare skin.

And, Love thought, *I need her.* His ex-girlfriend was the greatest naked beach dasher in the history of Oregon. She did it practically every time they visited the beach. Weather conditions never mattered. She usually had a bottle of Chianti with her, too, and a joint in her fringed purse.

Sometimes Love joined her. Sometimes he just stood back and watched. When he did, he knew he was looking at the very thing that made Oregon great, that she could do this, any time she so desired, for free.

Unleashing that Oregon greatness was the secret to defeating Ronald Ryan and the grasping wastrels of the land. It was the only way to win.

CHAPTER 22
THE SOBS

Ryan was right. The public had made a lot of noise. Now they had to be whipped into a revolutionary lather to crush the counterrevolution and Ryan's country club baronial assumption of their apathy.

Love drove out to the Mad Dog. West was sitting where he always sat, sucking on a Hot Mama. An episode of *Perry Mason* played in silence. It was the only episode where Perry lost.

West barely greeted Love. He was in a surly mood. He seemed defeated. He didn't have his fort of Rainiers around him.

"Why don't we just kill him?" said West, unprompted. "Political assassination's worked in the past. Look at Lincoln. The South got Andrew Johnson and the end of Reconstruction and Jim Crow for the next century. One bullet in Hitler's head in 1933 and no World War II. Look what we got when Hinckley botched it. Without Ryan, they're nothing."

Love was shocked. "Are you serious?" he said.

"Yes. I'd do it for Oregon."

Love believed him.

West continued: "Look what happened when McKinley was assassinated. We got TR, national parks and trust busting."

"We'd only make him a martyr," said Love. "Rich people would pour money into his cause. Besides, Oregonians need to win this battle. They've grown soft. So have I, you too. We've got to send a message and assassination isn't the message I'm after."

"Okay, you're right. But then how do we do it?" said West.

 "I know how," said Love. He waited a few seconds. "Rose, we need some Rainiers for the conference please."

Over the course of the next two hours, Love delineated his absurd strategy to obliterate Ronald Ryan and Santa Monica Dream's Coastal Entrepreneur Institute. West was silent but occasionally rubbed his hands together and broke into a devious smile at the mention of particularly far out stunts. At the end of Love's monologue, West held out his can of Rainier and clanked it against Love's.

"To the SOBs," said West.

"To the SOBs," said Love, tipping his Rainier.

He set the can back down after a long pull. "You better get the OTA for this," said Love.

"I'll get the OTA," said West.

"I need them naked."

"They'll be naked."

West got up from the stool and walked over to the window. He looked out to Yaquina Bay for a full minute, then returned to the bar. It was a strange series of movements for him, thought Love. Their work together was finally culminating and they had no idea what that culmination was going to be.

"Where are you going to be on the big day?" said West.

"On the beach in front of the Inn at Spanish Head," said Love without hesitation. "I'm going put thousands of people there and stage a circus that will blow Ryan's fucking mind."

Love put the call out again in perhaps the most unusual press release/poster/social media blitz in Oregon history. Love distilled the message to this: "Defeat the privatization of your beaches or Oregon is dead. Put your body on the line. This is war." He provided creative protest options and specific beaches to rally at. Clothing was optional. Ground zero was the beach in front of the Inn at Spanish Head. Time to party. Rally on July 7, the same day McCall had signed the Beach Bill into law in 1967. This was Oregon's real Independence Day.

Oregon had three months to prepare. Love cashed Ryan's check and spent it all on advertising, print, television, radio, digital, renegade handbills. They deluged the state.

The press went wild again, excepting of course, the *Oregonian*. The media was going to descend on Lincoln City and Love heard even the national networks were coming! Fox fucking News! All the talking blowdried heads wanted to set up exclusive interviews with Love the day of the protest.

"Meet me on the beach and you'll get your interview," he told them.

"The story's there."

A week after the call went out, Oregon State Parks called Love.

"We can't handle this sort of thing. It's getting out of hand," an official said. He was calling from a cubicle in Salem. He hadn't seen the ocean in a decade.

"Then get out of the way," said Love.

CHAPTER 23
TIME TO ROCK

Three months went by. Love wrapped up the school year and secured pledges of fealty from his students that they would hit the beach on July 7 and make a final stand for Oregon. Love gave them a sendoff for the ages and he knew they wouldn't let the Oregon gods down. "You want to make history, right?" he asked them. "You want Oregonians to be talking about you a hundred years from now, right?"

Yes, they wanted it. They'd wanted a great cause since their freshman year. Now they had one for the ages.

Love yelled: "I want forts, fires, sandcastles, cairns, haikus, face painting, running, jumping!

Send me pictures. Blow up my phone! Blow up the internet! Honor your Oregon forebears! Repeat after me: 'I love the smell of the ocean in the morning. That salty smell. It smells like victory.'"

They were primed for battle. They were ready to break on through. One look on their faces and you knew it was going to get hot. Finally, their generation had a purpose staring at them from three inches away. It was time to rock.

The rest of Oregon was primed, too. Love could feel it. The calls and messages and news reports kept building. There was movement out there. Something colossal was massing, ready to become a giant rogue wave eager to come ashore, break, spill, and wash away the filthy idea of private beaches in Oregon.

CHAPTER 24
SUPER SATURDAY

Super Saturday, July 7, arrived. It was a clear morning and the forecast called for sunshine.

Love walked Sonny down the beach at dawn and then fed her cold steak for breakfast. The old invalid husky would remain at home on the big day. She couldn't handle all the activity. But she would be waiting for Love upon his return—win or lose—and they would hit the beach again to conclude the monumental day and take stock of their lives as the sun set over the ocean.

It was nine in the morning when Love arrived on the beach in front of the Inn at Spanish Head. A hundred people and 30 dogs were already there. They all came up to Love. He addressed them from atop an ancient root wad: "Build me the greatest driftwood fort in Oregon history. Let's all work together."

And so it began.

A State Trooper came over to him as he was riding a huge driftlog being pulled by a team of harnessed huskies. Some ingenious dog owner had rigged it up.

"We won't do a damn thing to stop you," the trooper said. "Not even if you ransack the hotel."

Love shook his hand and looked down. The trooper wasn't wearing any shoes. He'd replaced his sidearm with a stick of driftwood. He drifted away and started building a cairn.

The fort rose higher. It became a command center. Hours went by. More people and dogs showed up. Food and drink started arriving. Restaurants were donating meals. Taverns were donating cases of pickled grotesqueries. Beer was everywhere, marijuana edibles, too.

Members of the media began filtering in; they looked utterly nonplussed. They didn't even know what nonplussed meant.

"Look at that!" someone yelled. Love stopped building and beheld a couple hundred people carrying guitars streaming south toward the command center. Behind them, 50 horses trotted in perfect military formation. The cavalry had arrived. Most of the riders were naked.

"No! Look at that!" said someone else, pointing to the ocean.

Sea lions were emerging from the surf. Dozens, then hundreds. They let off a raucous hosanna of grunts and barks and flapped and flopped their way to the command center.

"Wait, look at that," someone cried. Hundreds of men and women wearing Steve Prefontaine moustaches and nothing else were running toward Love. One of them carried a torch. They'd run a beer-soaked relay all through the night from Portland.

The Newport High School Marching Band appeared out of nowhere and launched into "Louie, Louie." The guitar army followed suit. Three chords can do a lot of good for the world if played with some conviction.

Love's phone was constantly beeping. He was getting reports and pictures from up and down the Coast. Thousands upon thousands of Oregonians were protesting on the beaches, or just having ribald fun, which amounted to the same thing. There was the world's largest hackey sack circle at Fort Stevens State Park. There were 3000 people and dogs at Short Sand Beach and a rock concert at the Matt Kramer Memorial. A surf band was shredding and whales came in close to listen. There was fire dancing around the Oswald West Memorial at the viewpoint off Highway 101 on Mount Neahkahnie. Traffic was blocked for 15 miles in either direction. There were 500 makeshift signs planted on Scalia's Gold Beach property; 400 of them broadcast the word "fuck" in some form or another. "Antichrist" was also popular. There was a man in a loincloth atop the Yaquina Bay Bridge, Oregon's crown jewel of New Deal socialism, waving an Oregon flag. There were people who just got in their cars and drove to the beach because they knew something unbelievable was going down, and they wanted to believe.

A reporter for the *NY Times* introduced himself to Love. He wanted an interview. There was no time for that; Love was building a fort! He suggested the reporter give it a try. He might better tell the story if he did.

Love sat down on the sand for a short breather. Several very tall men approached him. They were wearing the uniform of the 1977 Portland Trail Blazers' NBA championship team. Only they weren't wearing the shorts. He recognized them as Bill Walton, Lloyd Neal, Larry Steele, Bob Gross, Dave Twardzik and Johnny Davis. Walton had his arms over his head and circling them in a most curious way.

They came up to Love. Walton said, "What do you need?"

"Run me a perpetual three-man weave with driftwood, run it right through the television cameras."

"Rip City!" exclaimed the Blazers.

Someone tapped Love on the shoulder. Love, stood up, turned around and beheld a semi-circle of 15 naked OTA men. *For the love of God!* Each held a six pack of Rainier in one hand and a corn dog in the other. They had "SOBs" Sharpied green all over their bodies. They looked like berserkers, minus the blue.

One of them said, "We are at your service, sir. And more of us are coming. A lot more."

"Your job is to go talk to members of the media, television first," said Love.

One of the OTA crew cast a glance at a Fox News Blonde interviewing a sea lion. He smiled, then squirmed. There was unexpected but not unwelcome movement down below; it had been decades. He began walking toward the woman. She saw him and started backing up. He knew he had a dynamite line to deliver: "I've got a hard on for Oregon's beaches." His name was Butch.

It was two o'clock and 70 degrees. There was an ocean of people and dogs around Love. They kept coming.

They lit up the super fort. The fire rose higher and higher. It was a conflagration for a better Oregon. Kids started dancing around the fort and whipping at the flames with strands of kelp. Dogs chased them, howling and bellowing.

Somewhere up in his penthouse, Ryan was drinking wine and watching it all. He could not believe his eyes. Who were these people, these freaks? There were thousands of adults and children giving him the not-so-coded middle finger. He saw a dozen dogs sitting on the sand, pointing their upraised right paws to him. Dogs were flipping him off! He saw a hundred profane haikus ripping him a new one. He saw obscene sand sculptures depicting his shriveled manhood.

It was going to become an international spectacle. It would be ruinous to business. It would cost him money and influence. He fucking hated Oregon and their naked hippy socialism!

Then it started raining. In July. Ryan was soggy toast. Let him eat rain.

The ground beneath the Matt Kramer Memorial rumbled.

McCall wept.

Love was covered in sand and soot from the fire. He hadn't slept in three days. He'd subsisted on power bars and Rainier, and as of five minutes ago, fresh crab. He stared at the ocean. The breakers were rolling in white across a field of fading blue.

Then Love caught the scent of the fire; it smelled like victory. He heard the cracking open of Rainier; it sounded like victory. He turned around. It was West. He wasn't wearing any clothes and was holding a six pack of 16-ounce Rainiers. He broke one off from the plastic ring and tossed it to Love.

A black misshapen mutt stood near West. It looked like the canine equivalent of Lou Grant.

"Your new sidekick?" said Love, laughing and pounding the Rainier.

"Something like that. I got him at the shelter on the way over. Why not?" said West, smiling. It was the first time Love had seen him smile. It looked good on his face.

"What's his name?" said Love.

"Lou."

"Of course."

West held out his can of Rainier and Love clanked his against it. They nodded to each other.

It was time. Oregon had won, kicked Los Angeles' ass. It was rain over sun. Pallor over tan. Walton over Jabbar. People over greed.

Love shed all his clothes. He did more than that. He tossed them everywhere. About 7000 other Oregonians did, too. West bolted first, little Lou followed, Love took up the rear. He saw the *NY Times* reporter running, too; he was naked and appeared beatific.

Then the people and their dogs started running. There had been nothing like this in the history of the world or a scene like this in the history of world literature. Why not write it? Why not try to imagine a better world through fiction? Why not invent a new literary genre to imagine that better world? Why not invent pulp utopian detective environmentalist fantasy naked class conscious, socialist neo-realism polemical Quality Lit metafiction? (That could also serve as a textbook for an Oregon civics course.)

They ran to the ocean screaming and wouldn't stop until they plunged headlong into the waves. It was the Invasion of Normandy in reverse. Love was sprinting, zigzagging, pretending to stiff-arm all Republican/moneyed, anti-Oregon tacklers, and suddenly he felt someone catch up to him, nudge him in the shoulder.

It was her, the ex, naked except for the limpet necklace and smiling. She wore a ridiculous Chianti moustache.

Love slammed into a higher gear and passed her. She passed him a few seconds later and he yelled, "What took you so long?"

She just laughed her goofy, stoned, Chianti laugh. She was the one.

They dove in together, went underwater, and came up standing in a salt-crusted embrace.

"Will you marry me?" one of them said.

"Yes," the other said.

Fifteen minutes later they found a wandering druidic priest with a driftwood staff and it was done, in front of the smoldering remains of the fort, in a cloud of rosemary smoke, in front of friends, countrymen and Oregonians. The priest had brought along some bundles of rosemary branches for the protest and he gladly threw them on the embers. He pronounced Love and his partner married and then quoted Oswald West: "No local selfish interest should be permitted, through politics or otherwise, to destroy or even impair this great birthright of our people."

Amen.

The rain fell harder. Love and his partner kissed. She said, "Let's do this every year for the rest of our lives."

Love said, "Yes."

This book just became so-called romance documentary Edward Abbeyesque fiction. And a quasi activist coffee table book, too!

CHAPTER 25
SONNY

Ronald Ryan was never heard from again in Oregon. Santa Monica Dreams folded The Coastal Entrepreneur Institute and Ryan walked away from the Inn at Spanish Head. He stiffed his workers for thousands of dollars in wages. He held a fire sale to liquidate his properties along the Oregon Coast and lost millions.

West bought one, moved in, and started up his detective business again. Lou never left his side. He cut back on the Rainier, although not much. He refused to get a cell phone.

Antonin Scalia quietly disposed of his Gold Beach property. He continues to wreck the United States of America with his jurisprudence.

Love also bought one of Ryan's beachfront parcels south of Yachats and erected an unkempt complex of yurts, Airstreams and cabins. He dubbed it Fort McCall and it became a de facto retreat center for burned-out teachers who needed to make new fire. Love and his new wife rambled the beach five times a day, sometimes clothed. Sonny joined them in the morning until she passed away one winter evening snoozing by a burn barrel. The whole Oregon Coast mourned and thousands turned out for her service on Nestucca Spit. Love eulogized her as the greatest dog in the history of the Oregon Coast. Hundreds of thousands of words, ten thousand photographs, a coffee table book about her that became an instant Oregon cultural artifact. He was proud of that. He'd take that over an Oregon Book Award any day.

Love and his wife harvested limpets, built driftwood forts and cairns and sold rain in reality and metaphor. They transmitted good everywhere they went. That's the whole point of life, something the Ronald Ryans of the world cannot possibly fathom because their souls are empty, abyssal. They never transmit anything good; they simply transact money.

Love and his wife lived happily ever after. So did Oregon.

CHAPTER 26
A CALL TO ACTION

The Great Birthright is a work of fiction, at least 57 percent of it, but the reality is this: the horrifying scenario I describe of the US Supreme Court provided the opportunity to overturn the Beach Bill is plausible. In fact, I expect it. The signs are already here. Unless we Oregonians remain vigilant and petulant and far out on behalf of protecting this state's unique legacy of publicly-owned beaches, the great birthright will disappear.

How can you help? Social media posts and likes aren't going to work. Leaving the matter to elected statewide officials or the Oregon Legislature is a dubious strategy, too.

Supporting the watchdog efforts of the Surfrider Foundation, Oregon Shores Conservation Coalition and coastal watershed councils is one place to start. They all perform important work.

Someone should bring back the SOBs and really get wild with it. Maybe I'll do it. As Edward Abbey once wrote, "One brave deed is worth a hundred books, a thousand theories, a million words."

What Oregon needs is a ballot initiative that disallows any riprap footprint on any beachfront structure from advancing one inch seaward into public recreational space. No loopholes. This encroachment is already happening with multiple riprap permits and portends the next great fight for the soul of the Oregon Coast when rising sea levels threaten beachfront property. Just watch then how loud the rich owners cry for a public bailout. Their swinging hammock.

The war cry should be: *Never give an inch!*

These ideas are all well and good, but what Oregon truly needs to do is reaffirm its allegiance to the ideals of Oswald West's 1913 Open Beaches Act and the 1967 Beach Bill. Consecrate the bond again, publicly.

What better occasion than Friday, July 7, 2017, the 50th anniversary of the Beach Bill?

I propose here that on July 7, 2017 every Oregonian who cares about the great birthright skip work, chores and television and celebrate on beaches all along the Oregon Coast with friends, family, partners, dogs and perfectly weird strangers. Go Kesey on the sand! Make it 100,000 strong. Build forts and fires. Bring Rainier and wine and marijuana edibles and guitars. Make it the greatest Oregon public gathering since Portland celebrated the Blazers winning their only NBA Championship. Let the world know what our free beaches mean to us.

I'll be there.

Clothing optional.

AUTHOR'S NOTE:
THE SOCIALIST UNDERPINNINGS
OF A BOOK

The curious genesis and completion of *The Great Birthright* may interest some readers; I laugh when I think about it and thought the tale worth sharing here.

The book began in the spring of 2010 when I was teaching creative writing at Newport High School. I was taking my students through a rollicking unit on detective fiction, participating in all the various exercises to create a protagonist, antagonist, setting, conflict, etc., when the idea of a washed-up private detective from Newport investigating a potential threat to Oregon's publicly-owned beaches popped into my mind like the cracking open of a frosty can of Rainier.

During class, I invented my detective's name, Tom West, wrote a couple hundred words in longhand describing his personal life, and then abandoned the project once the unit concluded. At the time, I thought I'd never pick up the story again because fiction really isn't my forte, although I love reading it.

But I did stash all the pages and notes in my detective fiction unit folder and then buried it deep inside a black filing cabinet.

I had completely forgotten about the pages and notes when I reopened the folder two years later teaching the same unit to a different creative writing class at Newport High. I went through the exercises again and kept fleshing out West's character and the story's plot. I cranked out a few hundred more handwritten words and then stopped when the unit ended. Back in the folder and filing cabinet the idea went.

There it remained until the winter of 2015. I was teaching Freshman English at Astoria High School and unearthed the folder for a little creative writing fun. By this time, I had also read classic short stories and novels by Raymond Chandler, Dashiell Hammett, Jim Thompson, Mickey Spillane, Elmore Leonard and many new comical pulp fiction titles published by Hard Case Crime.

Perhaps that primed me.

I went through the exercises for the third time and the idea just exploded, the title, the thrusts of meta fiction, the politics, the polemics, my exponential loathing of Ronald Reagan, everything, literally in front of the students, projected on a screen as I wrote it in real time while they wrote their detective stories in their journals. I had never done anything like that before a class. I was giddy, typing madly, having fun, and claiming every ten minutes, "This is pure gold! Sheer lustrous gold!"

I wrote 7000 words in two weeks and then the unit concluded, but I didn't stop this time. I finished *The Great Birthright* two months later, all 40,000 words of it.

In other words, *The Great Birthright* was conceived and partially written while I was being paid by Oregon taxpayers. In other words, I benefitted from an unwitting form of government support for writers—call it socialism with a disguised face! What delicious irony: a book espousing the virtues of Oregon's socialist ocean beaches written with socialism-style support for the socialist-inclined writer.

Take that Lars Larson! Bring me on your bullshit show. Let me boast. Let's get down to it, asshole!

Now, for the ultimate irony to end *The Great Birthright*. According to the author Ron Perlstein, in his fantastic and searing biography of Ronald Reagan, *The Invisible Bridge: The Fall of Nixon and the Rise of Reagan*, when Reagan was running for President, he delivered a speech ripping liberal high school English teachers for replacing grammar drills with, "electives like creative writing, filmmaking, mythology, and detective story writing."

Such electives amounted to the socialist ruination of American public education.

Reagan was fucking right!

ACKNOWLEDGEMENTS

I had the pleasure of interacting with lots of great students at Astoria High School during the writing of this book, including a dope field trip to build driftwood forts. These positive interactions always make the writing go better.

Over the years, I've established some wonderful friendships with creative people that have informed and animated my writing about the Oregon Coast and its magical free beaches. These friends are: Tom McDermott, Andy Duffner, Tim Sproul, Angie Collins, Audrey Guerena, Bill Hall, James Herman, Tom Olsen, Don Frank, Leigh Oviatt, Nancy Slavin, Jack Harris, Mark Erickson, Dinah Urell, Rose DeBlock, Sandy Mummey, Tom Rinearson, Chanah Sheldon, Shannon Carson, Charlie Holboke, and others.

I thank my Oregon heroes: West, Kramer, Straub, Bacon, Bazett, Mc-Call. They preserved Oregon's beaches for me to come along decades later and find myself as a person and writer and teacher. I hope in some lasting way this book honors their service and keeps the heroic story alive.

Erin Labasan turned in another outstanding job as copyeditor and made several key suggestions for rearranging this book that dramatically improved it. Book designer Amira Shagaga and I continued our unique collaboration. My web designer Lena Burdett keeps everything humming online. I am greatly indebted to Cindy Popp for the wonderful print images that decorate the book. I must also thank CW for her unique contribution to this project. Dave and the crew at Pioneer Printing in Newport gave me yet another round of dependable customer service by producing their eleventh book for Nestucca Spit Press.

Nestucca Spit Press couldn't exist without the support of independent bookstores, libraries and readers that buy direct from me. Thank you.

I have two sets of the greatest parents in Oregon. They have been instrumental in my development as a writer and publisher.

Sonny, what can I say? We did it all together, every beach in Oregon. You were a living testament to the good a great dog can bring out in a person. I merely want to immortalize you to all lovers of Oregon's ocean beaches.

BIBLIOGRAPHY

Armstrong, H. Chester, *History of Oregon State Parks*, (Salem, Oregon State Parks, 1965)

Boardman, S.H., *Oregon State Park System: A Brief History*, Oregon Historical Quarterly, (Volume LV, September 1954, Number 3)

Cox, Thomas R., *The Park Builders: A History of State Parks in the Pacific Northwest*, (Seattle, University of Washington Press, 1988)

Gibbs, Jim, *Oregon's Salty Coast*, (Seattle, Superior Publishing Company, 1978)

Komar, Paul D., *The Pacific Northwest Coast: Living with the Shores of Oregon and Washington*, (Durham, Duke University Press, 1998)

Love, Matt, *Grasping Wastrels vs. Beaches Forever Inc.: Covering the Fights for the Soul of the Oregon Coast*, (Nestucca Spit Press, Pacific City, 2003)

McCall, Tom, with Neal, Steve, *Tom McCall: Maverick*, (Portland, Binford and Mort Publishers, 1977)

Olsen, Tom, *The Politics of Sand*, (documentary film), (Portland, Anchor Pictures, 2009)

Straton, Kathryn, *Oregon's Beaches: A Birthright Preserved*, (Salem, Oregon Parks and Recreation Branch)

Walth, Brent, *Fire at Eden's Gate: Tom McCall and the Oregon Story*, (Portland, Oregon Historical Society, 1994)

Oregon Highway Park System, 1921-1989, An Administrative History, (Salem, Oregon Parks and Recreation Department, 1992)

Matt Love lives in Astoria on the Oregon Coast and is the publisher
of Nestucca Spit Press. He's the author/editor of 14 books about Oregon.
In 2009, Love won the Oregon Literary Arts' Stewart H. Holbrook Literary
Legacy Award for his contributions to Oregon history and literature.
He's currently working on a book about his teaching career.
His website is www.nestuccaspitpress.com

GOODBYE OLD FRIEND.